Tackle Orienteering

John I. Disley

Tackle
Orienteering

Stanley Paul
London Melbourne Sydney Auckland Johannesburg

Stanley Paul & Co. Ltd

An imprint of the Hutchinson Publishing Group

17–21 Conway Street, London W1P 6 JD

Hutchinson Group (Australia) Pty Ltd
30–32 Cremome Street, Richmond South, Victoria 3121
PO Box 151, Broadway, New South Wales 2007

Hutchinson Group (NZ) Ltd
32–34 View Road, PO Box 40–086, Glenfield, Auckland 10

Hutchinson Group (SA)(Pty) Ltd
PO Box 337, Bergvlei 2012, South Africa

First published 1982
©John I. Disley 1982

Set in Monophoto Plantin

Printed in Great Britain by The Anchor Press Ltd
and bound by Wm Brendon & Son Ltd,
both of Tiptree, Essex

British Library Cataloguing in Publication Data
Disley, John I.
   Start orienteering.
   1. Orientation
   I. Title
   796.4′2   GV200.4

ISBN 0 09 145030 6 (cased)
ISBN 0 09 145031 4 (paper)

The paperback edition of this book is sold subject to the
condition that it shall not by way of trade or otherwise be
lent, re-sold, hired out or otherwise circulated without
the publisher's prior consent in any form of binding or
cover other than that in which it is published and without
a similar condition including this condition being imposed
on the subsequent purchaser.

Frontispiece: *Britain's finest orienteer, Geoffrey Peck, studies the map, consults the compass and keeps running through the forest: a man in balance with his environment.* Photo: Sunday Times

Contents

Introduction 6
1 First Time Out 9
2 The Orienteering Map 31
3 Events, Clubs and Courses 39
4 Clothing, Equipment and Routines 49
5 Using the Compass 57
6 Basic Orienteering Techniques 65
7 Getting Better – Additional Techniques 77

Appendixes
1 Useful Addresses 86
2 The BOF Badge Scheme 87
3 Additional Technical Information 89
4 Glossary 91
5 IOF Control Description Symbols 94
6 Permanent Wayfaring Courses 95

Introduction

The chances are that you already know, without realizing it, the principles of orienteering, and have put them to good practical use in your everyday life. Have you, for instance, ever studied road maps and checked the mileage between cities before you made a car journey, and then wondered if a detour to use a motorway would actually get you there faster? Have you ever stared at a London Underground map and counted the number of stations on the various alternative routes to your destination? Have you ever worked out an optimum route round a supermarket so that you can reach the checkout desk with your trolley loaded but without retracing your steps and wasting time and energy? If the answer is yes to any of these questions, then you already know what orienteering is all about – it is simple, intelligent navigation. Additionally, if you enjoy looking at road maps and searching for short cuts or trouble-free bypasses, then you are a 'map person' and will love orienteering. If you get quiet satisfaction from completing your shopping in record time – beating the system by intelligent route choice – then orienteering is your kind of game, and you certainly have the makings of a competitor in this fascinating sport.

Orienteering is a marvellous activity, combining that most natural of activities, running, with the puzzle of finding the best route through complicated terrain. This juxtaposition of the physical and the mental creates a totally satisfying recreation, particularly since the setting is one of dark green pine trees, purple heathland, golden carpets of beech leaves, or tumbling streams.

Now, before you read on, just a few words about the physical requirements. Orienteering is, of course, an activity carried out on foot, and events are held in fairly rough country, usually forested. You must expect to have to cope with uneven forestry roads, deepy rutted tracks and muddy paths. You will be asked to leave man-made routes and make your own way through the maze of trees and across heathland deep in heather. You will need to tackle small hills during the course and climb steep slopes out of valleys. You may have to cross fast streams and slippery ditches, wade through marshes, or clamber over fallen trees, decayed walls and rock outcrops. However, though I do want to convey the impression that orienteering is not a walk through a well-manicured park, let me reassure everyone by saying that there is seldom a course that traverses country too rough for an active grandmother or a lively ten-year-old. As long as you don't mind uneven ground, are prepared to get your feet wet and your clothes muddy, there is nothing to be feared. Certainly the first day of Harrod's sale is a far tougher proposition!

Most important of all, you can go round the course at your own speed, making up your own mind about whether you climb a hill or go round it; jump a stream or wade through it; keep to the paths or go directly through the trees. You can decide if you want to run from control to control, or jog, or even walk and enjoy the views. This sport's greatest success story is that it provides an activity for all. It offers the opportunity for real family participation: it's not just Mum and the kids watching Dad perform, or parents acting merely as chauffeurs to their sporting children. Everyone in the family from ten to sixty can enter an orienteering event at their own level of aspiration, and enjoy the experience within their own self-imposed limits of fitness and skill. After the race, everyone can assemble back at the car and discuss mutual experiences. All have been in the same navigational problem. No member of the family has been a drag on the others, nor have the ambitiously fit and energetic been an embarrassment to the slower members of the party. Orienteering is a good, healthy, outdoor exercise which can appeal to young and old and satisfy all the family's competitive ambitions, or even lack of them. This is the 'thought sport', with never a dull moment – the thinking person's answer to just jogging.

This book introduces the basics of orienteering to the beginner. Aware of the newspaper maxim that every picture is worth a thousand words, I have included a large number of illustrations. Orienteering is based on abstracting information from pictures on paper – maps – so the visual aspect of this book will provide a comprehensive view of the sport.

Necessary orienteering equipment is described, though in fact, apart from a protractor-type magnetic compass, very little specialist gear is needed by the beginner (see Chapter 4).

Like most sports, orienteering uses its own jargon. The most commonly encountered terms are explained in the text, but, to avoid breaking up the text too much, many of them will be found in the Glossary. So if you come across an unfamiliar expression, turn to page 91.

Of course, no book can really *teach* orienteering; only practice in the forest can do that. However, enough advice is contained in the pages that follow to see the beginner through from the complete novice stage to a good club standard. After reading the book, he or she will know how to find out where an orienteering event is being held, and have enough information to reach the starting line confidently and make a competent entry into the forest – perhaps even to find a few red and white marker flags bang on the nose. After that, there are other books and coaching courses available.

Dedication

To my mentor and friend Bjorn Kjellstrom who in fifty years of orienteering practice has been the inspiration that has enabled a Scandinavian gift to be shared with the rest of the world. Thank you.

January 1982.

Chapter One
First Time Out

What exactly is orienteering?

Orienteering is basically very simple. The event organizer goes out into a forest and hangs up some red and white flags on prominent features. He carefully marks the position of these controls on a large-scale map. Then the competitors, armed with a map and compass, go off and find the control marker flags. They start at one-minute intervals, and the fastest person around the specified pattern of controls is the winner.

Of course in practice it's a little more involved than this description suggests. Such a simplification is rather like describing football as kicking a ball through a goal mouth 8 yards wide – while forgetting to mention that there are eleven players trying to stop you, including one who can use his hands.

In orienteering there is no physical resistance from other players to impede your success. Not only is it a non-contact sport; often you will not see any of your rivals, either. It is astonishing how even a relatively small forest can provide hiding places for not only the marker flags but also hundreds of fellow competitors. Instead of another player or team providing the opposition, the competitors pit their wits against the course designer, who sets problems for them to solve. He ensures that they are presented with various choices of route between controls. We all know that a straight line is the

At the exact second of their start time competitors run to the master maps along the marked trail. Photo: Frazer Ashford

9

shortest distance between two points, but straight lines are seldom found in nature, and a direct compass bearing is not often the quickest way through a forest. It is the variety of choice, the many options on how to proceed, that gives orienteering its challenge and fascination.

Your first event

It is very important that you enjoy your first scrimmage with map, compass and forest. Read this description of a typical event carefully beforehand, and there is no reason why you shouldn't come away happy afterwards. But, unless you are a genius, your memories won't all be rosy. You will have had moments of sheer bliss when everything fitted and the red and white marker was hanging exactly where you wanted it to be, and there will have been long minutes when, to your chagrin, map and terrain were completely incompatible. But that is orienteering.

How to find an event

Events are usually held at venues well away from main roads, and you will have to write to or telephone local organizers, or the British Orienteering Federation (BOF) National Office (see Appendix 1 for address), to ask for details of fixtures. Once you have found your way to your first race, all other contacts are there for the taking – details of the next local event and of local orienteering clubs, and access to orienteering equipment. Better still, send 50p and a large (A4) stamped addressed envelope to the BOF for a current copy of their magazine *The Orienteer*. Apart from giving full details of all fixtures for the next couple of months, its thirty excellent pages of information also provide an insight into orienteering opinion and gossip. There are dozens of events all over Britain every year, and there is no closed season as such, so there is reason why you can't be at your first event in a few weeks' time.

When you get the information from the BOF, have a look at the fixture list. You will notice that every event has a grading, with a key to the various letters and figures at the top of the page (see page 11). You may be looking for a cross-country event – C; or a competition level of national badge event (see page 87 and Appendix 2) – C3; or a club or regional event – C4; or, better still, a 'Come and Try It' (CATI) event – C5. Obviously championships are not suited to the novice, but in three months' time, after gaining experience and joining a club, there is no reason why you shouldn't try this type of fixture.

This event, advertised to take place in the south-west of England, would be ideal for a beginner living in the West Country:

SW C5   Devon Informal Event. Kenton Wood (MR 912823)
C. Virgo, 37 Sandygate Mill, Kings Teignton
(Newton Abbot 60591) EOD

Here is all the information you need. The status of the event – C5; the map reference – MR – for the assembly/car park area; the address of the organizer; and the knowledge that you can enter on the day – EOD. All you have to do is turn up at Kenton Wood about 10.30 a.m. that day. Most events are held on Sundays, with a timespan of a couple of hours for start times.

What to take with you

Not too much: it's very likely that you already have nearly everything you will need for your first outing. Depending on the season, dress as if you were going to

---

A page from the official BOF fixture list, printed six times a year in The Orienteer

DIARY OF EVENTS

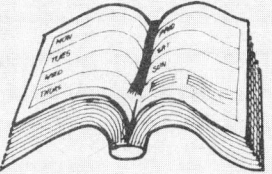

Copyright © British Orienteering Federation, 1980. No part of this list may be reproduced in any form without permission in writing from the Federation.

EVENT CODE:
C: Cross-country
R: Relay
S: Score
N: Night
U: Urban
X: Closed event
A: Assessment event

STATUS:
1: International
2: Championship
3: National Badge Standard
4: Club or regional
5: Come and try it (CATI), training

Entries on the day unless a closing date is given in brackets.
Telephone nos. in brackets refer to the town in the address.
Map reference **(MR)** given for car park/assembly area.

To receive further information on any event, send a stamped addressed envelope to the organiser.

	21st June
NI C4	**Gallopen III,** Moydamlaght Forest. D. Blair, 102 Shanreagh Park, Limavady. (4902)
SW C5	**Devon Informal Event,** Kenton Wood (MR.912823). C. Virgo, 37 Sandygate Mill, King's Teignton (Newton Abbot 60591)
	22nd June
NE C3(A)	**LO BADGE EVENT,** Crookbank. C. Harvey, 18 Townsend Crescent, Kirkhill, Morpeth, Northumberland. (M.3357)
WM C3j/C4	**OCTAVIAN DROOBERS JUNIOR & VETERAN BADGE EVENT,** Grendon. (MR.140/278978). Sue Bicknell, Langdale, Croft Close, Wolvey, Hinckley. (220411)
YH C4	**SYO Club Event,** Doncaster. K. Foster, 16 Barrel Lane, Warmsworth, Doncaster. (854386)
Scotland C4	**Borders School Championships,** Peebles. A. Hewatt, Education Dept., Regional HQ, Newton St., Boswells. (3301) (4th June)
Scotland C4	**Rosshire Event,** Munlochy. I. Bolton, Flat 2, St.Anns, Fortrose, Rosshire. (20124)
NI R4	**NWOC Relay Event,** Garvagh Forest. D. Blair, 162 Shanreagh Park, Limavady. (4902)
SE R4	**SN Relay Event,** Ruislip Woods. D. Colley, 1 Glenhurst School Road, Windlesham, Surrey. (Bagshot 73988)
	28th/29th June
NW C4	**THE CAPRICORN Long-O,** Eastern Lake District. A. Munro, 10 Haverholt Close, Colne, BB8 9SN. (0282 867852) (31st May)
	29th June
WM C4	**HOC Club Event,** Wyre Forest. M. Felstead, Plot 5, Catherton Road, Cleobury Mortimer, Kidderminster.
SE R4	**Havoc Relays,** Bedfords Park (MR.TQ.520924). R. Lynch, 2 The Avenue, Romford, Essex. (42137)
NI C4	**LVO Championships,** Doward Forest Park. A. Hamilton, 48 Botanic Avenue, Belfast. (46866)
SW R4	**Devon Relays,** Totnes (SWOA AGM). B. Till, 34 Halden Avenue, Teignmouth. (3600)

WREKIN ORIENTEERS

present

A Unique Badge Event on

THE LONG MYND
(by kind permission of the National Trust)

SUNDAY, 2nd NOVEMBER   Starts from 10 am to 12 noon

This event is included in the West Midland Gallopen
(It is proposed to make this an annual event).

Organiser: Dave Gittus
Planner/Chief Mapper: Peter Stephenson
Controller: Tim Goffe (EPOC)

MAP: Superb 1/20000 scale 5 colour 38-cm x 32-cm. 5m contours 25 square kms of previously unused 'O' terrain

LOCATION: Car Park SO 456973. Follow 'O' signs from A49 (one way system operating).
START: 1 km (allow 15 mins)
FINISH: Adjacent to car park.

COURSES: All usual badge Courses. The 'A' Courses will be longer than BOF recommended distances to make best use of this area.

CLOTHING: Remember the time of year and the open nature of the terrain (fell land between 600-1700 feet). Please dress appropriately.

ENTRIES to: Derek Turner
            The East Lodge
            Little Onn
            Church Eaton
            Stafford ST20 OAU

Tel: (Emergencies only)
     Wheaton Aston 841039

Two SAE required with entries, minimum size 9" x 4" for single entries larger and more postage for multiples.

Pre entries: By 18 October 1980

             Seniors £1.10p
             Juniors 60p

             Preprinted maps in strong polythene cases

EOD   Seniors £1.60. Juniors 90p
       Master Map System. No time allowance. Limited cover for Master Maps due to open terrain.

PLEASE HELP US TO HELP YOU

To: D Turner,
    The East Lodge, Little Onn
    Church Eaton, Stafford ST20 OAU

From:

Tel No:

Name	Class	Club	Preferred Start Time	Entry Fee
			TOTAL	

DON'T FORGET TWO x SAE 9" x 4"

An example of a publicity hand-out distributed at orienteering events

spend an hour or so walking energetically along country footpaths. I recommend an old tracksuit if you have one, or, failing that, a pair of old jeans and a long-sleeved T-shirt. Add an old jersey if it's chilly, and a light anorak if the weather is cold and wet. On your feet you'll need just a pair of jogging shoes – trainers – or a pair of old tennis shoes, or, quite functional, a pair of football or hockey boots. Whatever you do, don't buy anything yet. Wait and see if you like the sport first and then buy from the specialists – they have stalls at most big events.

You will need the following equipment: a red ballpoint pen to mark the course on your map; a black ballpoint; a plastic bag or case for your map (20 × 30 millimetres is the best size); a magnetic compass, if possible; and a whistle, to comply with BOF safety rules. The first four items will be easy, but the compass may present a problem. There is no doubt that, if you take up the sport, you will need a protractor-type compass; and even if you don't take to orienteering, it will come in useful for a lifetime of direction finding. Silva compasses are reasonably easy to find in mountaineering and scouting equipment shops, but read Chapter 5 before buying. You will also need to bring with you in your car (and it is advisable to come by car, since most events are held well away from the beaten track) the normal gear you would associate with exercise – a thick towel to dry yourself, and a change of clothes. There are seldom any changing facilities at orienteering events, so you will become expert at changing inside your car in bad weather.

Getting changed in the car is a skill strongly associated with the sport of orienteering. Photo: Sunday Times

You will appreciate something to drink, such as a thermos flask of hot tea, something to eat after your exertions, for most orienteering venues are some way from the nearest café or pub. In any case, you won't want to rush off immediately, because you will be anxious to talk about your route to fellow competitors and see your name appear on the results board. Most orienteering families make a picnic day of an event, since many car park assembly points are in delightful countryside.

Of course, you'll need some money to pay for your entry on the day. The fee can vary from 25p to £1; for this you will get the competition map and control card, and the results sent to you a week or so later.

Arrival at the assembly area

Your first piece of orienteering may well be to locate the assembly area – actually it shouldn't be too difficult, because the event organizer usually way-marks the route from the nearest main road to the car park: just keep a look-out for red and white signs and the magic letter O.

As you enter the car park – probably a farmer's field taken over for the day – you will see various signs such as Registration, Map Corrections, Start and Results. If you haven't arrived dressed for action, change now and go to the registration point. If you can't see a sign for it, just ask the first person you meet; you'll soon find that orienteers are very friendly and willing to help newcomers.

At registration – a car or small tent – you will have to make a decision: which course to do? You will be offered a variety of distances, ranging from a wayfarers' course of about 1.5 kilometres to the A course of 10 kilometres. There is no need to be a hero at your first event, so choose the wayfarers' if you are feeling insecure and unfit; if you really feel confident, however, then opt for a course about 4 or 5 kilometres long. But remember that course lengths are measured in straight lines from control point to control point, so that a course described as 5 kilometres (about 3 miles) could in practice, after a few detours for natural obstacles, soon stretch to about 8 kilometres.

So pick your course and pay your entry fee, when you will receive a starting time. Make sure it is far enough ahead for you to get yourself ready and to the starting point, which could be as much as fifteen minutes' walk away; ask how far it is. You will now be given the map and a control card, plus a control description list (for more information on these last two items, see page 16). Before returning to your car, ask if any map corrections are necessary: now and again the organizer has to ask the competitors to add some detail to the map because things have changed since it was printed – sometimes a new track is made or an area of forest is felled, or there is a patch of out-of-bounds to mark in where new trees have been planted. Copy any corrections carefully on to your map – a black ballpoint is best.

Preparation for the start

Ideally, you should now have a good half-hour to prepare yourself for the starting line. The following checklist will be useful:

1. Clothing and shoes – BOF rules require arms and legs to be covered.
2. Equipment – red pen, map case, compass and whistle.
3. Fill in the details on your control card twice – once on the card and once on the stub end.
4. Put your map, description sheet and control card in your map case.
5. Lock your car, hide the key, and set off for the start.

Map corrections are checked before leaving the registration area. Photo: John Disley

main-card   stub

```
YOU MUST HAND THIS CARD TO THE FINISH OFFICIALS
Please complete Card & Counterfoil — Name, Club, Class & Course
CLASS  /   COURSE  C   CLUB  N/A
NAME  Peter Williams
Have you got your: Whistle, map case, pen, watch, map, description sheet and ...
your SILVA compass. The sole distributors are:
Send S.A.E. for full price list.   SILVA COMPASSES (LONDON) LTD.
                                   10 THE CAUSEWAY, TEDDINGTON, TW11 0HE
                                   01-943 0315
```

FINISH 11-20-00   START 11-20-00   TIME

ONLY DETACH THIS COUNTERFOIL AT PRE-START

FINISH   START 11-20-00   TIME

CLASS: /   CLUB: N/A   NAME: Peter Williams

boxes for control punch

The control card with its counterfoil is usually collected at the registration point. Competitors fill in all the details except the start and finish times

After the first signpost you usually have to follow coloured streamers, which wind through to the forest to the starting point. You should now have some 10 minutes to spare before your start time is called.

The start is usually in a clearing with plenty of room for competitors to congregate and jog around for the last few minutes before the off. You will see that competitors are being called several minutes before their allocated start time. When the minute whistle is blown, they move forward towards the final line. On the way you will have your control card stub taken from you and your whistle checked. While you are waiting is a good time to examine the map again for its scale and the contour interval. Also check the map symbols and see if there is anything strange in the legend terminology. If there is, ask someone waiting with you for an explanation.

The start, and master maps

At last you are off – but where to? The first bit is simple: you follow a marked course for a few metres to the master map area, where you will find maps with the courses marked on them – but do check that you copy the right course. If you registered to do the D course, for instance, look for the D master map. Don't hurry: take your time and check that you have faithfully copied the circles on to your map. You will see that the controls are marked by a circle, the start by a triangle, and the finish by a double circle. Number your circles as per the master map, and join them carefully together in sequence.

You will certainly need to concentrate at the master map point, and the skill of fast and accurate copying needs practice. Others around you who ran forward at the same whistle blast will already be off their knees and bounding into the trees. Ignore them, and don't panic: stay where

Above right: *Waiting to be called to the start. The nondescript mass of forest needs the competition map to give it shape and identity. All will be revealed in a few minutes.* Photo: The Times
Right: *The start lines, with each class of competitor waiting in their own channel and progressing through at minute intervals to the actual start.*

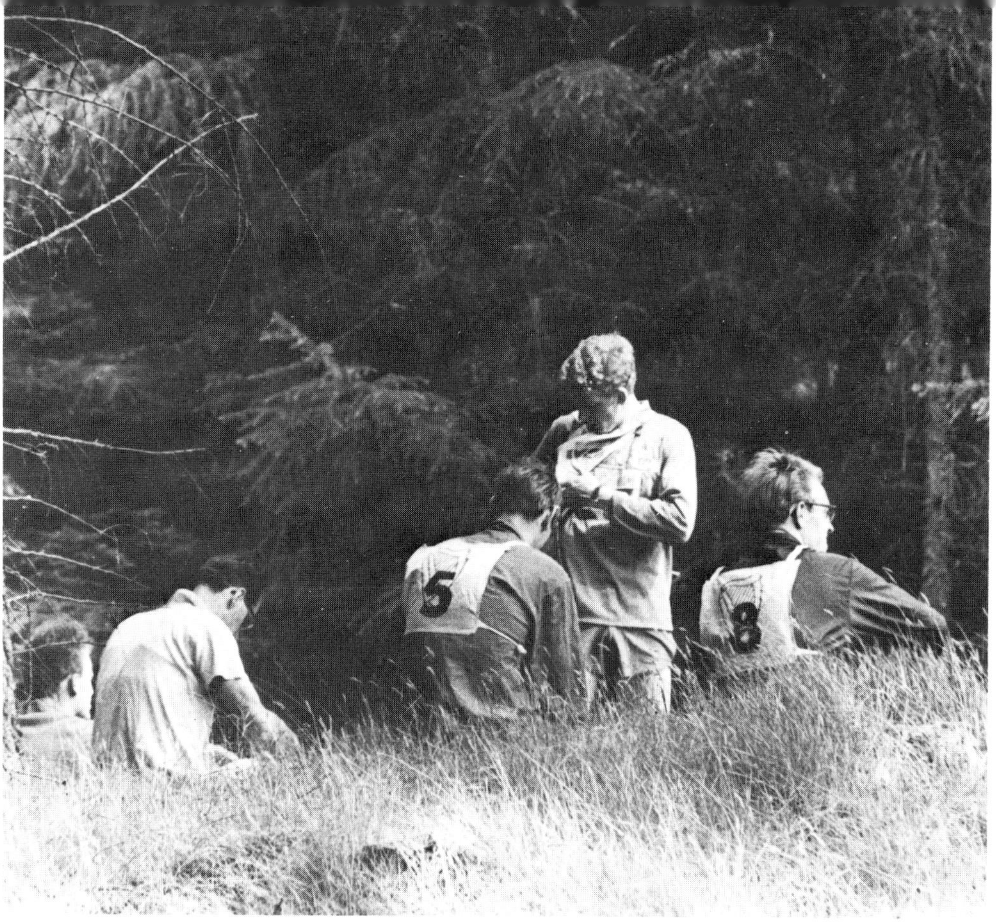

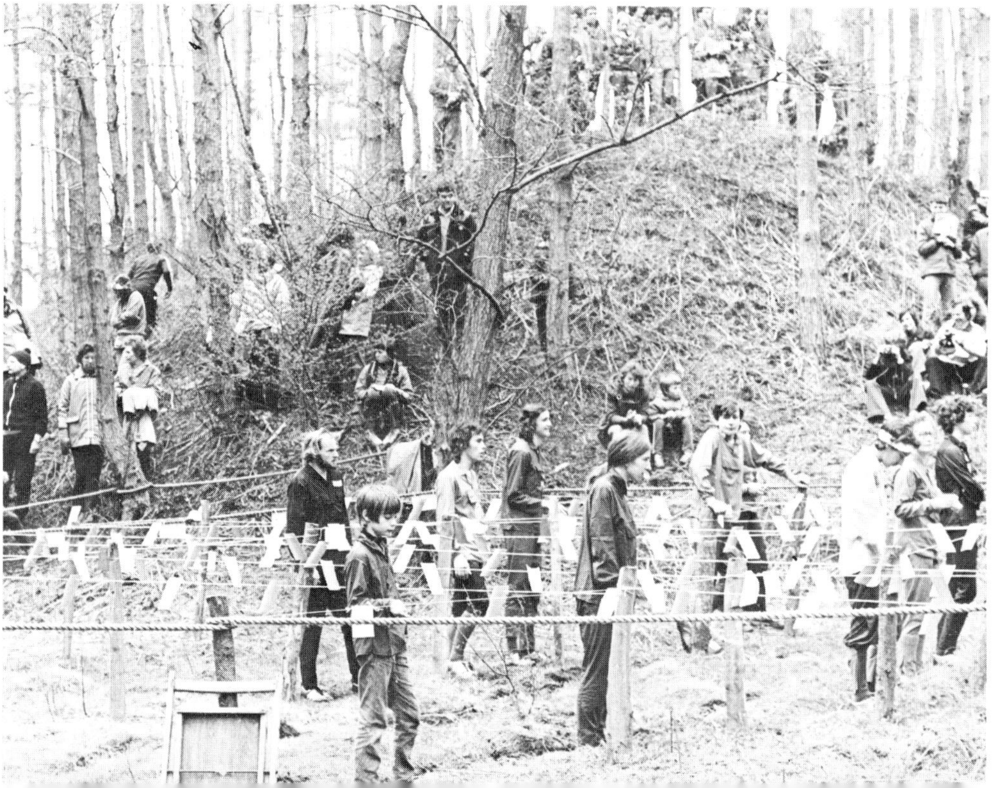

At important events the map is only handed out at the start time, but competitors are allowed to study its general format as they reach the last two minutes of the line. Here they can check for any symbols peculiar to this forest. Photo: Sunday Times

you are until you are sure that you have got it right.

You will find that the circles marking the controls are drawn around particular features on the map. Find those marks on your map and put your circles carefully around them. Make your circles about a centimetre across, so it will not be difficult later to see the details around the controls. Now check again that you have numbered the controls correctly, and joined them together in the correct order as shown on the master map.

You can now stand up and tackle the next problem – how to find those features surrounded by red circles.

Off and running free

Now you are on your own. You know where you are on the map – at the middle of a triangle, which on the ground seems to be a clearing in the forest.

In order to explain graphically some of the more fundamental techniques of survival in relation to this first competition, let us imagine an enthusiastic first-timer talking or thinking to himself. Orienteers do in fact talk to themselves in the forest quite often – advising caution, reminding themselves to check the control code, or telling themselves that all is not lost because one control has proved hard to locate.

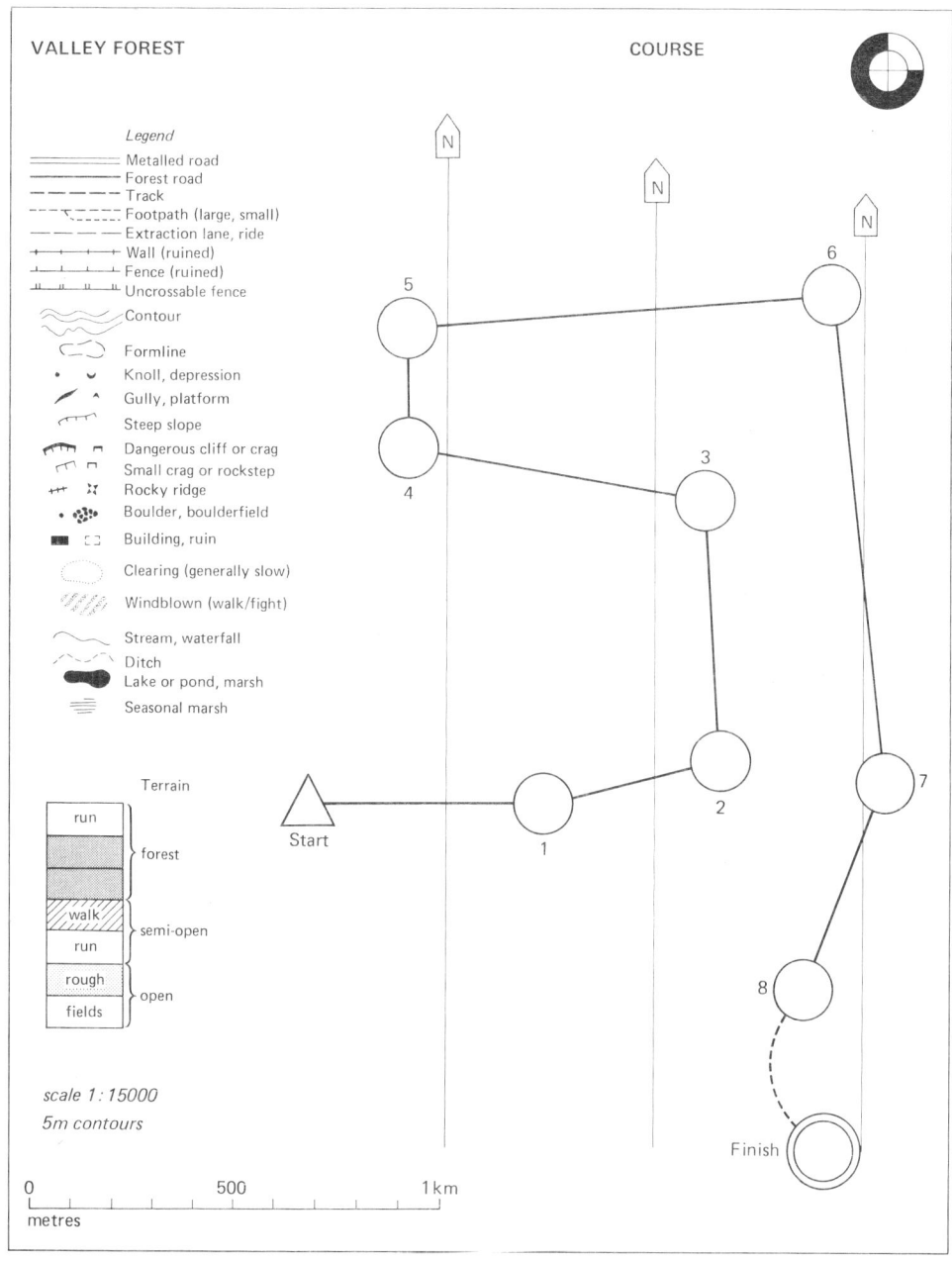

The master map will look something like this simplified version. All the circles and lines joining the controls will be in red to stand out from the detail of the map

It is essential to copy faithfully all the information on the master map. A mistake here can spoil the day. Photo: The Sun

Right, so Control 1 is on the right – that means to the east of the start. How far is an inch? Let's find the scale on the map – it's always given. Here it is – 1:15,000. Well, that doesn't help too much at my level of experience. But wait, there's a visual representation of the scale, a black and white line depicting 100-metre sections. Now I can see that an inch is about 400 metres. That's not very far. Shouldn't take more than four minutes at normal walking speed. That seems simple – due east for 400 metres. How am I going to find east? I'll look at the compass needle, which always points north, and then turn smartly right.

So the novice pushes into the trees at the eastern side of the clearing. He needs some resolution to break through the branches. Progress isn't impossible but it certainly isn't pleasant, and further-

more it's a bit lonely there. Where have other competitors gone? Surely some of them must be aiming at the same control? So he halts and has another look at the map.

There must be a better way than this. What does the map show immediately to the east of the clearing? Oh, yes – I seem to be in some dark green, and dark green patches mean fight, so the going is tough here. I don't like it much. I think I'll go back and start again, and in future steer clear of green areas. In any case, I think I should try and find some tracks and paths and get the feel of this map. If I strike north I'm bound to cross a big track, and then I can turn right and head towards the east. When

The master map area has the tension of the examination room just after the question papers have been given out. Here a group of youngsters ensure that their red circles are drawn around the correct features on the map. Photo: The Guardian

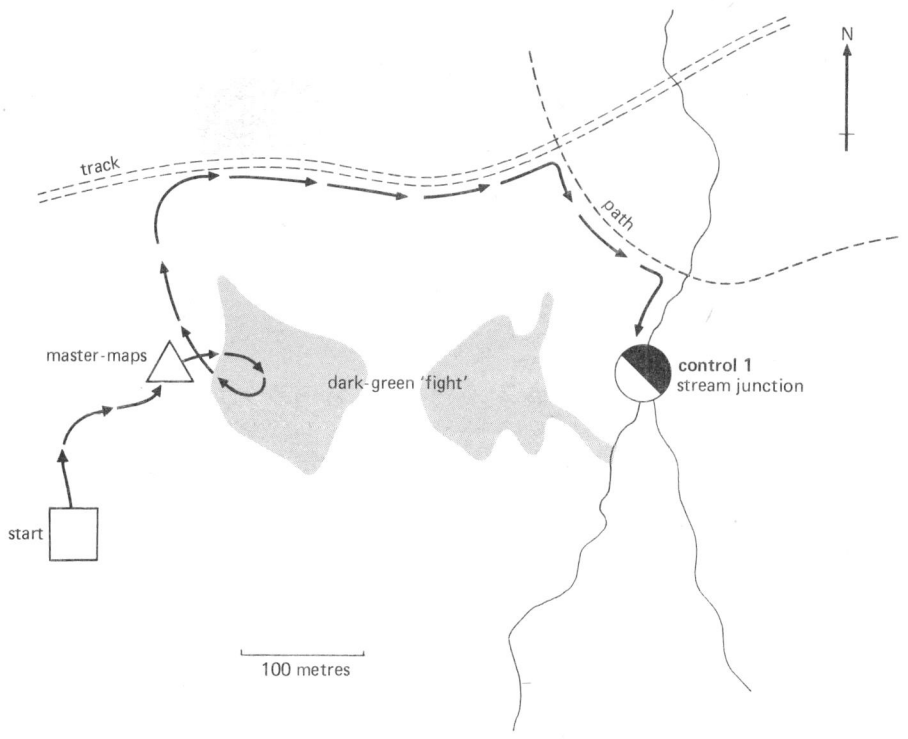

The navigational start to the event is always at the centre of a triangle on the map. The disastrous excursion into the dark green fight area was wisely abandoned and a safe handrail route devised round to the north of a direct line to Control 2. This route is twice as long when measured on the map, but many times quicker than a beeline through unpleasantly thick forest

I get to that path crossing the track I can turn right again and continue till I reach the stream, then turn south, and the flag should be just a few metres away.

Now our orienteer is beginning to think: getting the feel of the map is important. Even champion orienteers are cautious on the way to Control 1, and try to find a safe route that uses handrails to guide them to their destination. The example above is a classic situation where the straight line is not the best route between controls. The fight areas will discourage any attempt to go through them on a compass bearing, and, although it would be feasible to navigate around the green jungle to hit the stream directly from the west, the more sensible solution, particularly for the novice, is to go around three sides of the rectangle and come down the stream into the control from the north. The track, path and stream all act as handrails, and the going underfoot will be fast for most of the route. It may look half as long again as the direct route, but it is by far the quicker choice in practice. Back to the novice thinking out loud again.

Look at the footprints at the side of this stream – I'm not the first orienteer to use this route. Steady – there's the stream junction and there's the red and white flag. My first control. I think I can congratulate myself, apart from that mistake in the dark green: I've used my brains to solve the problem. What next? Well, I have to prove

Dark green on the map means head-high undergrowth and doesn't encourage fast progress. Photo: The Times

```
┌─────────────────────────────────────────────────────┐
│ COURSE "C"        5.1 km      180 m climb           │
├──────┬──────────┬───────────────────────────────────┤
│ No.  │ Code     │ Description                       │
├──────┼──────────┼───────────────────────────────────┤
│ 1.   │ AD       │ Stream junction                   │
│ 2.   │ CS       │ Depression                        │
│ 3.   │ CE       │ Pond - east side                  │
│ 4.   │ ST       │ Re-entrant                        │
│ 5.   │ VB       │ Boulder 2m                        │
│ 6.   │ DS       │ Knoll 3m S-side                   │
│ 7.   │ TA       │ Fence corner                      │
│ 8.   │ XX       │ Earth-bank S-side                 │
└──────┴──────────┴───────────────────────────────────┘

Follow tapes 250 m to Finish

Course closes at 1500 hours by which
time all competitors should have
reported to the Finish whether they have
completed the Course or not
```

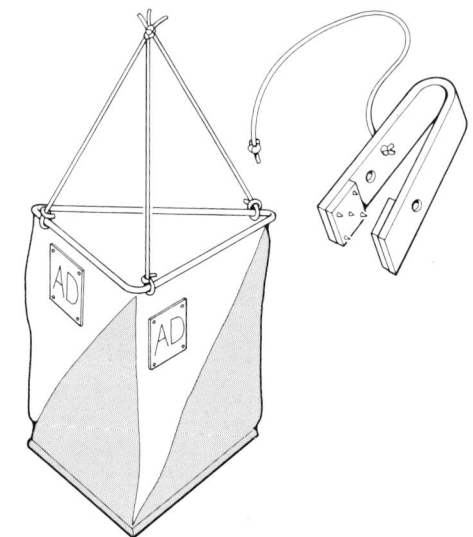

The control description list is a definitive document giving all the information required about the course and the positioning of the control flags

The control flag is a prism with each face 30 centimetres square and divided diagonally into red and white areas. The code (AD) is marked on the flag. The pin punch produces a pattern of holes when applied to the appropriate box on the control card

that I have found the control : but before I stamp my card perhaps I should check that I've found the correct flag, so I must look on the control description list. Control 1 – stream junction AD – is marked, and there on the corner of the flag is the code letter AD. It's the right one. Now I have to mark box number 1 on my control card with the pin punch that's hanging from the flag.

Terminology in orienteering is quite specific, and you will need to discover exactly what is meant by the brief descriptions (see Appendix 4). Some of them, like 'stream junction', for instance, are self-explanatory, but others such as 'platform' or 'niche' will have to be learnt. Every flag has a code boldly displayed on or near it, so that you know whether it is the one you are looking for; when there are several controls in the same area of forest, it is essential to check the code. To make a code check before punching is a good habit to acquire right at the start of your orienteering career. Nothing is more frustrating than to be disqualified

because you stamped at the wrong control. Now, on to the second control.

Where is it? It seems to be a bit further east and not very far, and there are no green bits between here and there. I should be able to manage 300 metres in a straight line without getting lost. Check again on north, look over my right shoulder and go straight ahead. This bit of forest is quite easy to run through. A few sections of undergrowth to bypass, but there's no problem because I can see quite well through the tall trees.

Can I have missed it? I must have covered 300 metres by now. Perhaps I should look again to see what I'm aiming for. It says: 'Control 2 – depression (CS)'. I suppose a depression is a hole in the ground. That means that it won't be easy to see unless I'm fairly close to it. I'll go on a bit further and swerve to the right. Perhaps that last lot of brambles pushed me too far to the north. But even so there's no sign of a flag. Okay, I'll cut my losses

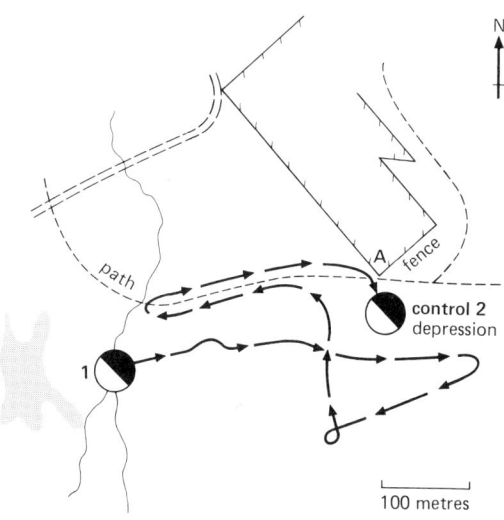

100 metres

The attempt to run roughly eastwards for 400 metres failed to locate the depression or the marker flag. A fresh start was needed, and the best catching feature was the path crossing the area to the north of the control. By retracing the route westwards to the path/stream crossing, an exact position was found. Then the fence corner at A was carefully reached, and the last 50 metres south taken at a watchful walk

and go back to something I can recognize. But there's an orienteer over there. Perhaps he's at a flag – my flag. ...Well, this is where he was standing – but there's nothing here. What does the map say? I can't be badly lost. I'm in this section, south of the path that crossed the stream near Control 1. If I go north, I can be caught by the path, then turn back westwards until I meet the stream. Then I'll know where I am again.

Another important lesson – when you are lost, don't waste time thrashing about in the forest: go off and find something easily recognizable and start again. The path in this case is the feature to the north, and will enable the beginner to re-establish contact with the map and begin thinking again.

Right, here's the path – but at which

point am I on it? Maybe it's best to go right back to the stream so that I really know where I am on the map. So – here's the stream again. But I was here fifteen minutes ago. Where did the time go? This bit is only 300 metres long! I have to retrace my steps along the path eastwards until I'm opposite the depression, and then turn off. How do I know when to do that? Look at the map. That fence corner on the north of the path is almost exactly opposite the control. I'll jog to that corner and then go in very carefully. I think it's called an attack point.

Now I must keep my eyes open – 50 metres is not very far. However did I miss it last time? The depression is obvious and the flag plainly visible from 20 metres away. So much for my ability to stay on a straight line. I must have veered south all the way from the stream. Obviously I've got some homework to do before my next event.

Our beginner is picking up the jargon of the sport: 'attack point' is the term given by orienteers to an easily recognizable feature that is close to the control; at their best they are track junctions, field corners or boundary features. When the orienteer reaches the attack point, he changes down into bottom gear and proceeds the last few metres alertly and cautiously until he sees the control. There is more information about such techniques in Chapter 6.

Hullo – I've got company. Yes, it's that middle-aged lady I met in the car park – the one who said that she walked all the way round the course. Well, she's walked faster than me to reach this point, because her start time was well after mine. If I stop making stupid errors, I can easily keep in front of her from now on. No vague wanderings; stick to tracks and real things I can see and touch.

Now, what about Control 3? Seems straightforward – back to the fence corner, then turn right along the path to that junction just a few metres away. Then the path goes nearly all the way to 3. It seems

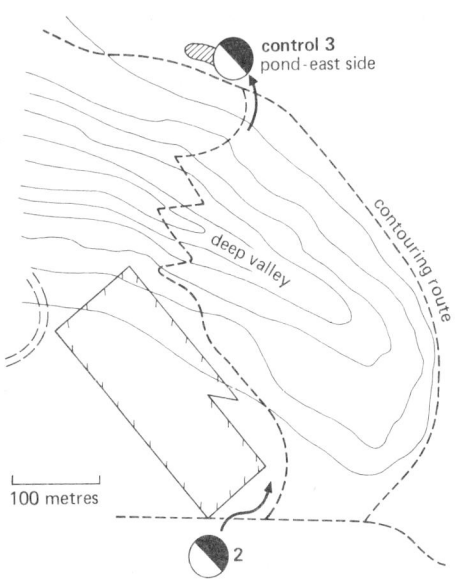

The nearest handrail path was not in this case the best buy, because it descended steeply for 30 metres and then climbed back up to the plateau. The alternative contouring route to the east is longer but gives level travel on a good surface

to zigzag a bit, but it's continuous and all I have to do is follow it. Where it hits that track is nearly at my control – that blue mark. Must be a pond – I can't possibly miss that. Let's run. Good, it's going downhill, pretty steep. I can see why it zigzags – to reduce the gradient. I'm in a valley. I don't like the look of that uphill slope ahead. It seems longer going up than going down. My leg muscles don't care for this too much.

Made it with just a couple of rests, and here's the pond. But who's that by the flag? It's her – the walking Wonderwoman! How did she get ahead of me – levitation? Maybe there was another route?

Look at the map. She must have seen all those V-shaped brown lines across my path. She recognized them as contour lines and didn't fancy climbing 25 metres. She walked round the valley rim on that path to the east. Twice the distance, but

obviously half the effort. Next time I'll know better.

Our intrepid beginner is already appreciating that brute strength isn't much good in orienteering, and is learning all about the hare and the tortoise. He, the hare, rushed blindly off down the hill towards the control, only to be stopped dead in his tracks by a steep climb out of the valley floor. The tortoise used her brains and calmly walked around the head of the valley on a good path without raising her pulse.

The next four controls are found without too much trouble. A brief excursion down the wrong arm at a track crossing, as a result of holding the map the wrong way up, is soon corrected when a field is reached that should have been a metalled road. The walking lady always seems to turn up at the control, but seldom from the same direction as the novice. She appears better organized at the control, too: checked, punched and away before he has even got his control card out of his map case. Obviously some forethought is needed, and he resolves to give it some thought.

I've only got one more control to find, and I don't seem so tired now as I did back at Control 3, either. Might even manage a brisk trot to the finish line. Right – what problem has the course setter given me this time, from 7 to 8? It looks as if I shall have to cross this 'semi-open land', a sort of heathland and coloured a dirty yellow on map. No paths over it. No helpful paths either side. Better consult the map again. 'Control 7 – earth-bank – south side (XX)'. I can't miss this earth-bank: it stretches right across the far side of the semi-open land... This must be the bank – it's 3 feet high. No control in sight. Wait a second – what side am I on? The north? Well, the description says south side, so over we go. Still no flag. What do I do now? Another look at the map.

Is there any feature beyond the control that I can use to pinpoint where I am on this wretched earth-bank? Nothing – just the line of the forest starting again. Think. If I turn left and search the bank that way, is there anything that will tell me that I've gone too far? Hopeless – I just fall off the map! If I turn right, is there any feature I can use to find out where I am? What's this V next to the earth-bank? It's a pit – exactly what I need, and so far west that I can't possibly have got myself on the far side of it. Well, I've finally worked something out for myself – used my head to save my legs. I'm off to put that last control in the bag.

He turns right (west) and is rewarded

A control is located. The control card is punched, while the orienteer is already searching the ground ahead for the best route to the next control. Photo: Tom Astbury

Good technique at the control can save minutes during an event and gives less time for other competitors to be helped by your presence at the flag. Photo: Tom Astbury

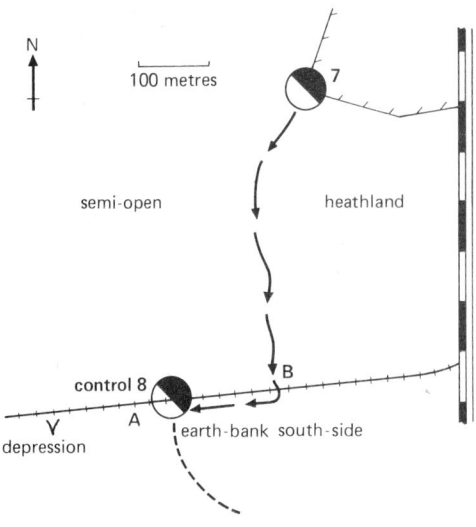

The heathland between these controls is featureless and the linear earth-bank equally lacking in positional information. The edge of the map discourages any search to the east, and sensibly the only other feature besides the actual flag was looked for first – the depression. If that had been found first, it would have been obvious that the earth-bank had been reached at point A, and that the flag must be further east. In this case the flag was found before the depression, as the earth-bank had been located at point B

by finding the flag before he reaches the pit. Now all he has to do is to follow the coloured streamers for a couple of hundred metres to the finish. Despite his many errors, he's obviously orienteering material. At the earth-bank he responded to the challenge of solving a problem by looking at the available evidence and applying logic. Actually, he could have applied his logic more productively deciding before setting out across the semi-open area which way to turn when he reached the earth-bank. Orienteers know from experience that keeping to a direct line across featureless country is almost impossible, so they automatically aim to one side of a control on a particular feature. Then, when they reach the linear feature, they know exactly which way they need to turn to find the flag. They call this simple and effective technique 'aiming off'. It will be discussed more fully in Chapter 6.

This is very satisfying – running in to the finish with all the controls marked on my card. Hand it to the official – keep the map and description sheet. It's taken two and a quarter hours – no wonder I feel a

The run in to the finish from the last control is usually along a marked route and provides an opportunity for that last expenditure of energy. Photo: Frazer Ashford

The results are always a centre of attention in the finish area.

bit weary. I certainly covered more ground than the 5.1-kilometre length of course – must have been twice as far. I wonder if two and a quarter hours is a reasonable time? I'll go and find the results area and see what the other times are like.

That's impossible – 42 minutes 11 seconds is the best time on the line. No, I don't think it's a mistake because there are another dozen names with times inside fifty minutes.

Well, I suppose I was a bit languid at the master maps, and then there was that hiatus in the green jungle. I must have lost ten minutes, at least, there. I wasn't too clever at Control 2 either – had to go back nearly to 1. I remember the hill that added some time to my effort – I bet the winner didn't exhaust himself on those zigzags.

I didn't really do too badly for a first time – I can explain at least an hour away due to sheer inexperience. But my time is still almost double that of the winner.

The post-mortem session – the reappraisal of the course – is a vital part of orienteering. Errors are catalogued and explained away, clever short cuts are recalled with pride. There is no doubt that, when standing by your car and looking at the course again on the map, the whole thing looks deceptively simple. Our beginner has already started to rationalize his mistakes: next time – oh yes, there's definitely going to be a next time – he won't make those mistakes again.

Back in the car park, he is already engaged in an inquest with the walking lady. 'Yes, I saw you at Control 2,' she might say. 'You just walked right by the flag. You were staring ahead and never looked to the side. I always turn right round when I think I'm near the control site, and by this simple manoeuvre I saw the flag that peripheral vision had missed.... And why didn't you go in a straight line from 4 to 5? Didn't you see the power line marked on the map? You had to look carefully for it in the trees, but it was there and there was a cleared ride under it – there usually is under power lines; that's why I look out for them.' The beginner can learn a lot by talking to an experienced orienteer.

Chapter Two
The Orienteering Map

The map is the key that unlocks the secret doors to the route. Without its detailed picture of the terrain, the forest would remain a confused mass of light and shade. It is possible to spend many happy or frustrating hours exploring its complexities without ever taking it into the countryside. A good map can be as absorbing as a well-written novel.

But of course the map isn't fiction, and it has to relate uncompromisingly to the terrain it depicts. During the past ten years, orienteers have devised a common international system for showing various features on a map; they have agreed on what constitutes such features as a knoll, a stream, an earth-bank and a vegetation boundary, and on a common set of symbols that indicate such features. This means that, once you have memorized these symbols, you can read a competition map anywhere in the world.

Specific requirements

The best maps, charts or plans are those which have been drawn to meet a fairly narrow special requirement. Such maps are kept simple and to the point, and carefully avoid unnecessary details. The orienteer's task is fundamentally how to navigate on foot. Unlike the rambler or the mountaineer, he is not interested in information such as the names of farms, streams or hills, nor does he wish to

Map held firmly in the left hand and compass gripped with the right, an international competitor races to the Finish along the marken trail. Note her loose but protective clothing.

know about battle sites, parish boundaries or National Trust property.

The white and green on orienteering maps express the reverse of what they traditionally mean on topographical maps. Since most time is spent in forested areas, it is logical to keep these regions free from visual obstructions such as colour; a coloured background is therefore only used to indicate fields (often out-of-bounds) and open areas such as heath and moorland. Patches of ominous green are used to denote the various intensities of fight in thicker areas of trees, but no experienced competitor would do more than use the edges of these green patches as navigational aids.

Other colour screens – dots and bands – are designed to show runnability and visibility in the forest. White denotes that the going underfoot is reasonably fast and that vision through the trees is good. Sometimes visibility can be fine, but clogging bracken, heather or brambles can make the going tough. Understanding the relationship of the various green and yellow screens on the map to the actual terrain is a skill which needs experience to develop.

Much of the discussion that takes place after a competition is centred on the efficacy of the map, and how far it was judged to be an honest interpretation of the terrain. The International Orienteering Federation has listed the following six requirements for orienteering maps.

Map reliability

Maps should be up-to-date. Forests, particularly modern spruce plantations,

31

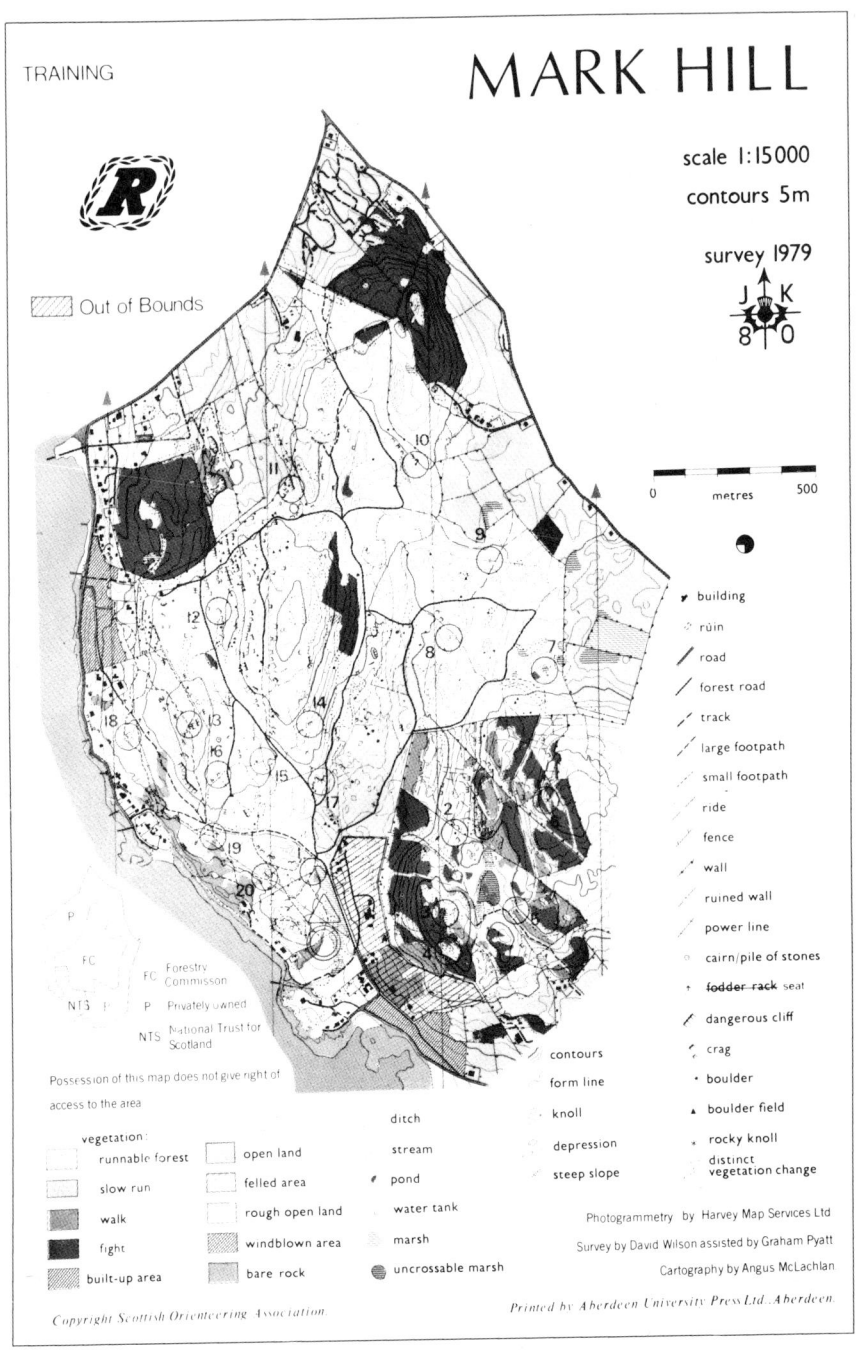

This modern orienteering map (reduced – original 260 × 170 millimetres) shows the standard format for well-produced maps. It has a title, legend, scale and contour interval information, and credits the surveyors and draughtsmen. This particular map is overprinted with control sites laid out for a training event

Open forest where the going is good underfoot is white on the O map. Difficult areas with low-branched trees, thick brashings on the ground, or dense undergrowth of brambles or rhododendron thickets, are in various shades of green. The darker the shade of green, the worse the conditions

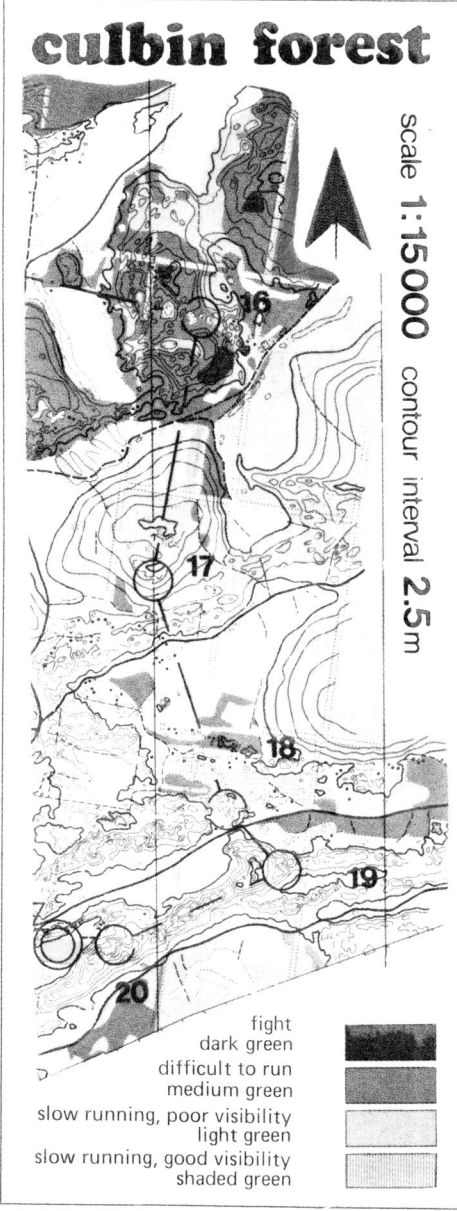

change rapidly in accordance with forest management – felling, making roads and new planting. Nature, too, can take a sudden hand in altering the environment with wind and flood. Seasonal changes to the undergrowth are also important. Bracken at the height of its growing season in July and August can make an area impenetrable. Mappers working on a championship map must produce one that it consistent with the seasonal growth expected at the date of the competition. Significant post-printing alterations to the forest must be brought to the attention of the competitors by map corrections displayed before the start.

Map detail

The map scale must reflect the character of the forest and the nature of the competition it is drawn for. Scales from 1:20,000 up to 1:5000 should be selected in accordance with the detail needed to ensure competent navigation. Paradoxically, more detail does not always mean greater clarity and ease of navigation. There is a point at which additional information confuses the issue. A good map is often characterized by what is omitted from it. For instance, it is pointless mapping in a depression that is 2 metres across when it is just one of scores of similar pits in an area; all that is necessary is to indicate by the appropriate symbol that this area of terrain is pitted. However, one small depression on its own in an otherwise featureless part of the forest should be included on the map. The basic criteria for including a feature on a map are that it will:

    (a) assist navigation in broad terms;
    (b) provide intermediate checkpoints in sparsely featured areas;
    (c) provide additional navigational points around a control site;
    (d) give the opportunity for a wider choice of control site; and

(e) provide extra information to establish the orienteer's position in the forest.

Running feasibility

Orienteering is all about route choice: consequently, the orienteer who leaves the tracks and paths must have reliable information about the runnability of the forest. Just as he knows that tracks provide secure footing, he must be able to abstract from the map the potential 'friendliness' of the ground under the trees. A suitable balance can then be maintained between navigating across the forest and running around on paths.

Readability

The mapmaker must remember that, despite the addition of necessary fine detail, the fundamental picture of the area should still stand out clearly. Small 'point' features should not hide the main structures. Linear features such as tracks, paths, boundaries and streams must always stand out clearly from the mass of detail. Similarly, the shape of the land should be instantly apparent from the configurations of the contour lines.

The magnifying lens which is built into a protractor-type compass is a great help, but intelligent route choice decisions should not demand the eyes of a hawk.

Where there is too much detail on a map many orienteers, particularly those whose sight is less than perfect, may abandon any attempt to map-read and instead press on with a compass bearing. That is not good orienteering – expedient, perhaps, but it does not create navigational challenge and excitement.

Out-of-bounds

The map must indicate clearly all areas that are out-of-bounds to the orienteer. This includes all property where no permission to orienteer has been sought or granted. Gardens in the forest, young-tree nurseries, fields with crops (grass is a crop at haymaking time) are all in this category.

Out-of-bounds also applies to dangerous areas. Old mineshafts, quarries, steep cliffs and deep marshes must all be clearly marked. A solid red line denotes the extent of the out-of-bounds area; this mark is reinforced by red diagonal-band shading across the forbidden area.

It is also important to note that the possession of an orienteering map does not give you the right to make use of the forest, unless it is publicly owned. Permission for many orienteering events is negotiated only on a one-off basis with the owners. This does have an advantage – the existence of private land ensures that forests remain unknown to orienteers and so available for important championships in the future.

The legend

The basic IOF-accepted map symbols should be used at all time. However, local peculiarities sometimes need a special symbol, and in such circumstances it should be explained in the margin.

Map symbols

The various symbols are very easy to learn. If you can already read ordinary

---

These internationally accepted orienteering map symbols are very rational, and the modern five-colour map allows features to be displayed and identified very clearly. For instance, all water features are in blue and forms closely related to contours tend to be in brown; man-made features such as tracks, paths, fences, walls and buildings are in black. Most countries need some special symbol to denote a feature not on the IOF list, and the UK variants are shaded in the legend here

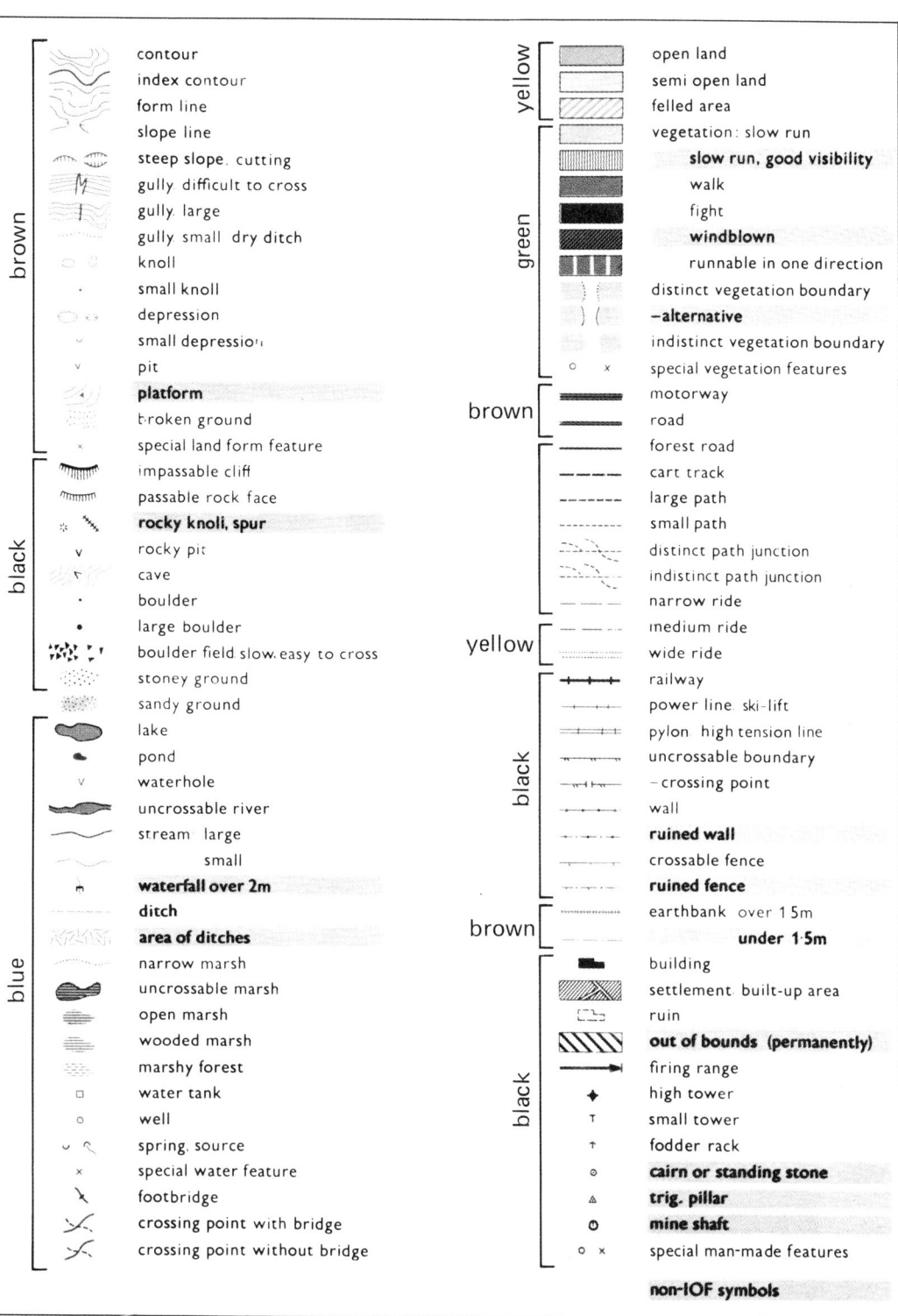

topographical maps, such as the Ordnance Survey, you will recognize many of them. The new symbols are as visually explicit as the mapmaker can devise, for his object is to enlighten, not to confuse. You should be able to master them after just one hour's study, but don't worry if a few signs elude you at first, because most orienteering maps reprint the legend in the margin.

Map scale

Orienteers need far more detailed information of a particular kind than is normally included on a topographical map, which is why they make their own maps.

The novice described in Chapter 1 would have noticed at least three major differences between a normal Ordnance Survey map (1:50,000 – 1¼ inches to the mile) and the orienteering map. The most obvious difference in the orienteering map is its large scale – 1:15,000 (about 4 inches to the mile). The other distinctive features are that the map is drawn to magnetic north, and that, as already mentioned, the forest area is white rather than green.

The mapper needs plenty of space to draw in essential marks clearly, so large scales are always used – things happen quickly on an orienteering run. Of course, it isn't necessary to identify every feature on the ground as you read the map on the run, but with such a large-scale map there is no excuse for losing contact with the course. Every few seconds, your position can be confirmed by identifying a new feature.

At this stage we need to start relating millimetres on the map to metres on the ground. The conversion is very easy: scales are indicated by figures which show how many units on the ground are compressed into one unit on the map. A scale of 1:10,000 means that 1 millimetre on the map equals 10,000 millimetres on the ground, or, to be more practical,

A change in scale from 1:20,000 to 1:10,000 quadruples the actual area of the map, which allows far more detail to be clearly drawn

1 millimetre equals 10 metres, or 1 centimetre equals 100 metres. Most orienteers have a good visual impression of 1 centimetre, and, by just crossing off the last two zeros from the given scale, they instantly have a figure in metres for distance in the terrain depicted by 1 centimetre on the map. Of course, doubling the size of the scale from, say, 1:20,000 to 1:10,000 actually quadruples the space given to the mapmaker. Maps of complicated terrain, and training maps for beginners, are usually drawn to a large scale of 1:10,000 or even 1:5000, to give very clear detail.

Map contours

After checking the scale of the map, the orienteer needs to note what the contour interval is on the map that day. The contours – the brown lines that give form to the linear features drawn on a map – are usually drawn at 5-metre intervals. Every fifth line is drawn a little thicker than its neighbours, so that 25-metre differences in height can be easily recognized. But mappers do vary the contour interval, depending on how hilly the terrain is, so it is essential to check each time a new map is studied.

How the map is produced

In the early days of orienteering, competitors had to make do with rather crude copies of Ordnance Survey 1:25,000 scale maps. The photostatted black and white copy map gave just enough information to enable the sport to become established. There were more blank areas than mapped sections, and it was always exciting crossing the uncharted parts and wondering if contact would ever be made again with the map.

Year by year, orienteering maps have become more professional, but by and large they are still produced by orienteers themselves. Many orienteers are fascinated by the process of surveying and drawing maps, and have become highly proficient cartographers. The British Orienteering Federation holds an annual competition for the best British map of the year; the winner receives the Sir Francis Chichester trophy, which is the compass from *Gypsy Moth III*.

Today's maps are based on aerial photographs subjected to photogrammetric treatment. The base maps are usually drawn at twice the scale of the intended final product. They have the bare bones of the finished maps accurately plotted, as well as the contours for the major features; tracks, major paths, streams, walls and fences are drawn in to provide the framework for the necessary final details. The filling out of the base map is achieved by hours of legwork in the forest. Sometimes this is done by one dedicated individual, but more often the hundreds of hours' work required are shared by a team. All small features like knolls, pits, ruins and changes in vegetation are carefully plotted in relation to the fixed features on the base map.

It is then handed over to the draughtsman in the team, who carefully draws or scribes on sheets of plastic – one for each colour to be used – all the assembled details. Every effort is made to ensure that the information provided by the various members of the team is consistent. The printing itself is done professionally. The names of those responsible for the map are printed in the margin, so we know who to thank for the pleasure, or sometimes anguish, that the map generates. Many orienteers help to make maps during their careers and get a great deal of fun in the process. Incidentally, there isn't a better way of learning about relating a map to the ground than by making one yourself.

Direction on an orienteering map

Orienteering maps are not meant to last a lifetime, and can get seriously out of date after a couple of years as a result of forest management, natural growth, the public and nature. But the fact that they are updated frequently means that it is possible to draw the map to magnetic north without producing a long-term discrepancy. Magnetic north shifts a little each year, so that traditional topographical maps, which are intended to last at least ten years, need to be drawn to grid north, which is constant. However, this means that compass bearings have to be corrected before they match grid direction – a complication which can slow down map-reading.

No such problem exists with orienteering maps. North on the map is in line with the compass needle, and no corrections or adjustments are necessary when co-ordinating the use of an orienteering map and compass. Now and again you may find that you have to orienteer on an OS map, in which case it will be necessary to take note of the difference between magnetic and grid norths. Some of the more massive O events in the mountains, for instance, use ordinary maps, and the simple solution to the declination problem is explained in Appendix 3.

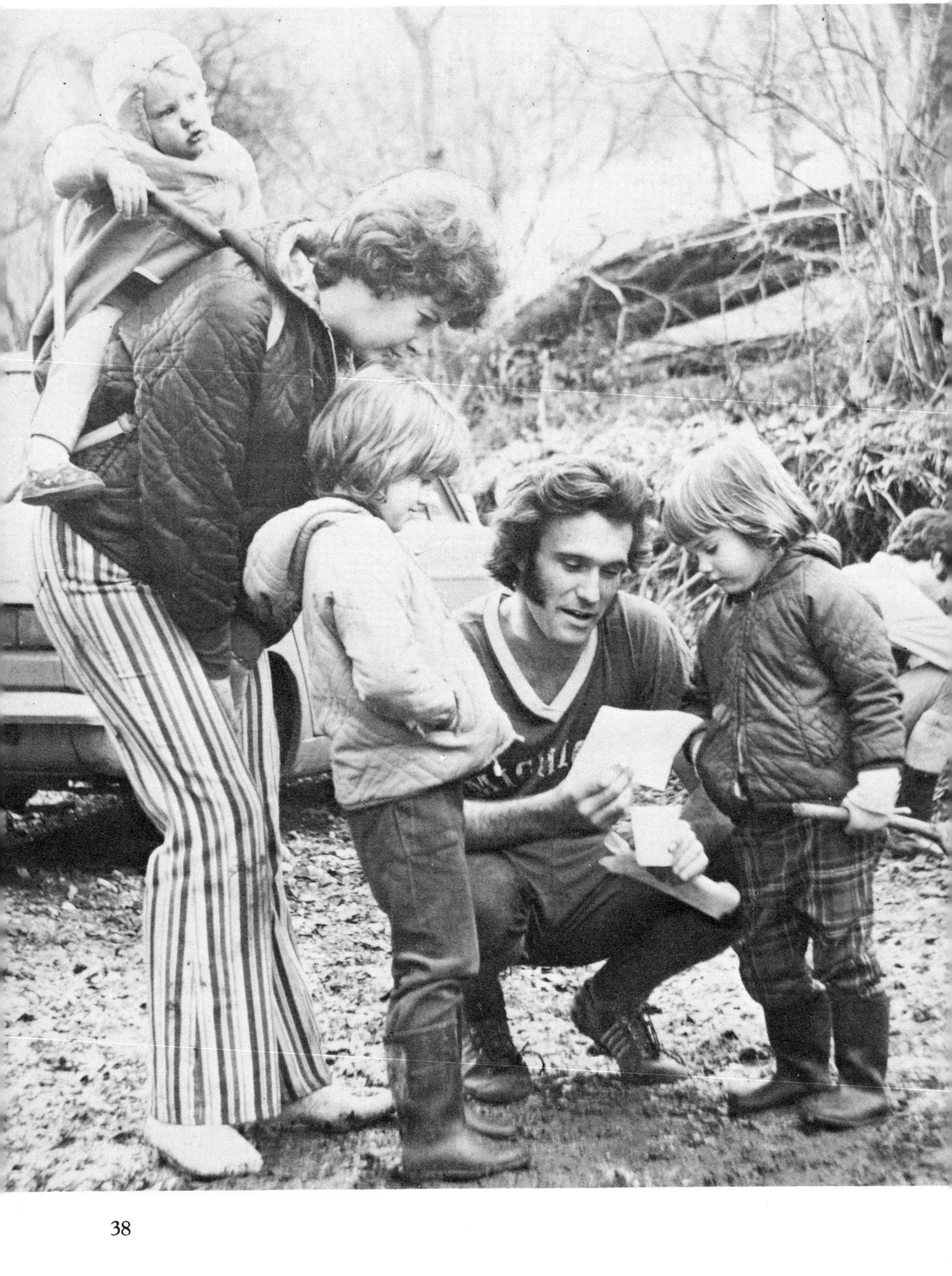

Chapter Three
Events, Clubs and Courses

Orienteering events come in all shapes and sizes, but all of them are designed to provide a fair challenge for all ages and ambitions. Although there are local and one-off variations, the great majority of competitions have the same structure.

What event?

When the BOF office sends you, as mentioned in Chapter 1, information on local events, it will include a fixture list for the next three months, attached to which is an explanation of the event codes – the letters and numbers that precede the events in the list. It looks like this:

Event Code	*Status*
C: Cross-country	1. International
R: Relay	2. Championship
S: Score	3. National badge standard
N: Night	
U: Urban	4. Club or regional
X: Closed event	5. Come and try it
A: Assessment event	(CATI)

The novice orienteer is welcome to compete in any event other than the international and championship categories. Similarly, he will be well looked after at cross-country and score events.

Club registration

The sport is essentially organized on a regional basis – nine English regions, plus Scotland, Wales and Northern

A family about to set off around the wayfaring trail. Photo: J. Gillett

Ireland (see Appendix 1). Once you are committed to becoming a regular orienteer you will need to join one of the many clubs that run the events. Your communication from the BOF will also give you the name of your nearest orienteering club, but during your first few events you will no doubt meet orienteers from different clubs and be able to select a club based on the encouragement of your new friends.

The membership system is simple. One single annual subscription affiliates a member to his club, the regional association, and the British Orienteering Federation. Membership entitles the orienteer to compete in all events on the BOF fixture list. Other benefits include a bi-monthly copy of *The Orienteer*; a regular regional newsletter; third party insurance cover when you are competing; a vote at the General Meetings of the Federation; access to coaching courses for personal performance, map-making and course planning; and a comprehensive advice and information service from the national office. Subscriptions vary from one region to another, but the annual fee in 1982 was around £10 for those aged nineteen and over. Other forms of membership are available for those under nineteen and for family groups.

What course?

The selection of courses on offer at the registration point can seem a little confusing at first, but it is just this variety that gives orienteering something that other sports often lack. The way that people of all ages can compete is one of the best aspects of orienteering, and competition is divided among eleven age groups from the age of ten up to the over fifty-sixes.

Age classes

Class	Winning Time (minutes) Championship	Badge event	Distance (kilometres)
M 10	30	27	2–3
M 11–12	35	32	2–3
M 13–14	45	40	2.5–4
M 15–16	55	50	3–5
M 17–18	65	59	4–7
M 19–20	75	68	6–10
M 21+	90	81	10–14
M 35+	75	68	7–12
M 43+	70	63	6–10
M 50+	65	58	4–7
M 56+	65	58	4–5.5
W 10	30	27	2–3
W 11–12	35	32	2–3
W 13–14	40	36	2–3.5
W 15–16	50	45	2.5–4
W 17–18	60	54	3–5.5
W 19+	75	68	5–8.5
W 35+	65	58	3.5–5.5
W 43+	60	54	2.5–4
W 50+	55	48	2.5–4
W 56+	55	48	2.5–4

The prefixes M and W denote men and women. The time in minutes indicates an average winning time for that class. The distance in kilometres is an indication of the probable length of course

Your age class for a calendar year is based on your age on 31 December of that year. For instance, if you are nineteen on 22 December, you will have to enter in the M 19 or W 19 class for the whole of that year.

The recommended times and distances in the table relate to championship events, either regional or national, and badge events. Club events would have times and distances about 20 per cent under the championship figures.

When the entry numbers for a particular age class become too large the organizer splits the field, usually on the basis of past performances, and makes an A and a B and sometimes even a C class. These additional categories are given slightly easier courses than the A courses.

In category 3, 4 and 5 events it isn't necessary to provide separate courses for the different age groups and sexes. Usually there are just five or so courses – A to E – and by some judicious arranging of the lengths of course good competition can be enjoyed by everyone with a minimum of strain on the organizer.

Course	Appropriate Age Classes	Average Length (kilometres)
A	M 21	about 11
B	M 19; M 35; W 19	about 8
C	M 17; M 43; W 35	about 5.5
D	M 15; M 50; M 56; W 43	about 4
E	M 12; M 13; W 13; W 15; W 50; W 56	about 3

Types of course for category 3, 4 and 5 events

Colour coded courses

There are some disadvantages in having to compete within your age group, particularly in small events which can be regarded as training opportunities; consequently for club events a colour code system is being used more and more, which always relates to a level of difficulty that is not totally dependent on the length of the course. In hilly, difficult terrain a blue course (the hardest) may be just 7 kilometres long, the same length as a medium-difficulty course – green – would be in an easy forest. Once the colour code is understood it is easy for orienteers to pick a course and know what they are getting.

Colour	Type of Course	Average Length (kilometres)
White	Easy, with obvious controls	up to 3
Yellow	Longer, but still easy control sites	3–4
Orange	Rather more difficult controls	4–5
Green	More difficult and longer	5–6
Red	Difficult controls but not too long	5–7
Blue	Hard and long – for the experienced	7–12

The colour code

Wayfaring courses

All age class and colour coded competitions are run against the clock. Competitors start at one-minute, two- or three-minute intervals and are timed at the finish to the nearest second. However, there are many orienteers who are not attracted to competition at all, and prefer to solve the puzzle of navigating through the woods in their own good time. This sensible group have the option of entering what is called the wayfaring course.

Wayfarers register at an event centre and, just like their competitive colleagues, receive a map, control card and description sheet. They usually have their own start and finish area, well clear of the hurly-burly of the racers. The courses are fairly short and the controls are usually in the more pleasant parts of the forest, near tracks and paths. Often the organizer arranges for the wayfaring route to visit good viewpoints and interesting features.

Wayfaring courses are excellent for families and ideal for teaching young children the skill of reading maps and identifying features. Very often parents use this course as a post-competition opportunity to do some coaching with the youngsters before going home.

Wayfarers set off on a relaxed stroll through the woods. Photo: Sunday Times

The BOF badge scheme

The Federation operates a very popular badge scheme which is open to all members in every age class. To win a badge you have to reach a certain standard in three competitions: the standard for gold, silver and bronze is based on a percentage of the average of the first three competitors home in your age class. As the value of the badge increases, so does the level of the percentage.

Championship badges can only be earned by performances made in championship events. Appendix 2 contains more details about these awards and the standards that have to be attained.

Course documents

The control card

This is a vital document in orienteering, because it confirms that everyone who went into the forest has come out safely and checked in at the finish. The card is in two sections and you enter your details on both parts. The smaller stub section is collected from you just before you start, and is finally reunited with the main section in the results tent.

Because the card is a safety check it is essential to hand it in to the finish officials whether you complete the course or not. A search party looking for someone who is already at home drinking tea is going to be frustrated and annoyed.

Although the control card's format may vary slightly from event to event, the actual details are constant. The figure on page 43 depicts a typical control card.

You will probably be expected to fill in most of the details yourself, after registration and before the start. Normally the start time you have been given will be written on the card by the official who registers you and takes your fee. You will need to add all the other relevant details, such as your name; club, if you have one; age class; and the course code – age class, letter or colour. This information must appear on both portions. The cards are often in different colours, related to the various courses, so don't worry if the next card you see isn't like yours. In major events such as championships, the control card is actually overprinted on to the map together with your name, start number and class.

Most of the card consists of space for the boxes where you will make the mark that proves you have visited the control flag. This is done by punching the appropriate box with the pin punch that hangs from or near each control marker (see page 44). These pin punches produce different patterns of holes on the card, and officials back at the results tent use a light box to check that the overall pattern is correct. The organizers don't expect the punch marks to be dead centre in the box, but it is helpful if you can make a clean mark and in the box – not overlapping its neighbour.

Control description sheet/list

Depending upon which course you select, you will receive a small piece of paper with the descriptions of all the controls that you are expected to locate (see page 43). The information on these sheets is most important and is designed to help you in your search. First, it tells you what you are looking for at the centre of the red circle – track junction, ruin, or re-entrant, for instance. Second, it provides the code number or letter of the control, so that you can confirm that you have indeed found the particular flag you are looking for.

These lists are fairly consistent in their format and language, so that no ambiguity arises about the information they give. The only problem that the beginner will find when looking at the list is to relate a physical shape and dimension to a verbal description. Most of the features used as control sites are extremely simple – tracks, paths, streams, ditches, walls and fences are all linear features which are easy to identify. Free-standing objects such as boulders, cliffs, ruins and ponds are equally easy to visualize and identify. However, you might need some experience in the field before becoming adept at recognizing in the flesh such features as platforms, knolls, spurs, gullies and depressions.

All the control sites are precisely indicated by symbols on the map (see page 94).

The pictograph system

An approved international system of signs has been designed to replace words in the description sheet, so that orienteers can compete easily all over the world. Learning the new language can be fun, and may sometimes be necessary as more and more important events are changing over to the pictograph system. The full list of pictographs is reproduced in Appendix 6.

Control sites

Course planners are always recruited from the ranks of experienced orienteers

The description list shown in words on page 24 looks like this when displayed in the pictogram system

	C	5·1 km.	180 m.
1	AD	⌇	Y
2	CS	⊖	
3	CE	∪	○
4	ST	∩	
5	VB	▲	2
6	DS	●	3 ○
7	TA	⋀	Y
8	XX	⤢	○
	○------250------▶◎		

– poachers turned gamekeepers for the day. But in fact there is no competition between the orienteers and the course planner, who is a kind of groundsman concerned with marking out the playing area to ensure that the competition is both challenging and fair.

Planners spend many days in preparation for the event. Much of the praise for a successful course will relate to the control sites, and on how they are selected for variety and position. The planner will take a lot of trouble to describe the controls accurately, and even more trouble to ensure that the control flags are hung exactly where they are described. If the control description says 'The stream bend', for instance, I would expect to get my feet wet when punching my card. I would lose confidence in the organization of the event if the flag was hung just 5 metres away on a convenient tree branch.

Once you have navigated to within sight of the control feature indicated on your description sheet, you should be able to see the marker flag without trouble – unless, of course, the description tells you that the flag is hung on one side of the feature. The flag should also be hung at a height where it is as visible as a competitor punching at the flag, which means that the markers are not stuffed down rabbit holes or suspended in the middle of a thick rhododendron bush.

The marker flag is three-dimensional with red and white faces split diagonally (see page 44). Different ways of hanging the controls and positioning the pin punches are shown below.

Types of orienteering competition

Cross-country

The great majority of events are called 'cross-country', and in this book the

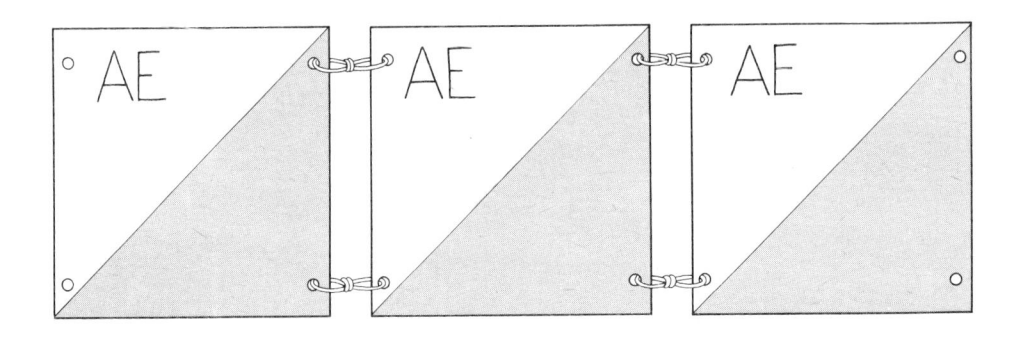

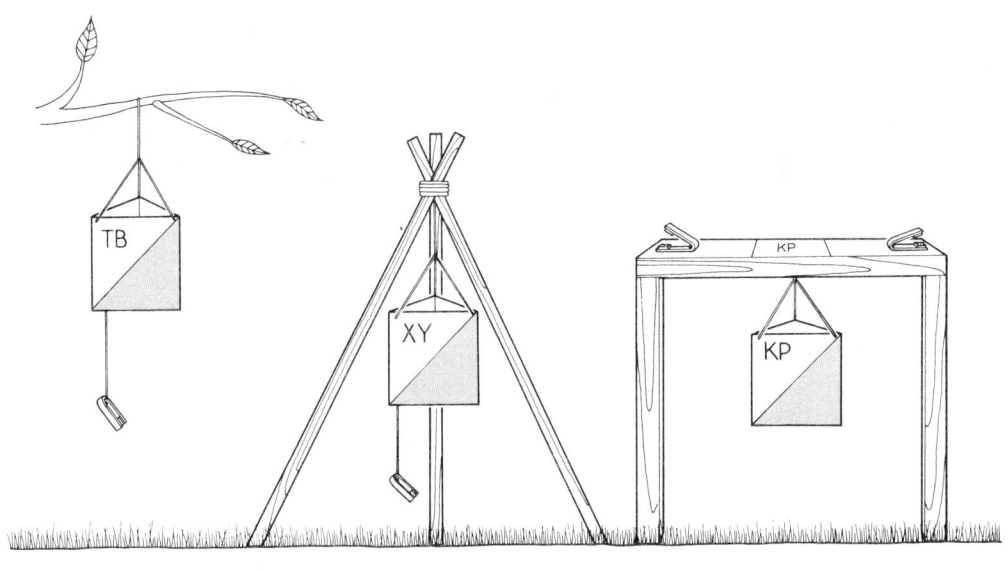

The flags are always hung on or as close as possible to the feature described. The pin punch is either hung from the flag or fixed to the gantry that supports it. The last few controls often have several punches to avoid crowding, but they all have the same code of pins

---

descriptions of events and situations have so far all related to cross-country competition. If the expression has any meaning in the orienteering context, it is that the course from one control to another – but not the actual route – is prescribed, unlike an athletic cross-country race where everyone follows the exact course and route laid down by the organizer.

You will find that the pattern of starting at timed intervals and following a prescribed circuit against the clock is what occupies most of your time as an orienteer.

Score events

In this kind of event, which is excellent for training, there is no set course to follow. The competitor devises his or her own pattern of collecting controls. There is a time limit for the event – perhaps sixty or ninety minutes – and in that time as many controls are visited as possible. As you might expect, the controls that are furthest away or most difficult to locate are worth more points than those near at hand and on obvious features. To encourage competitors to return within the appointed time limit there is a penalty points system geared to minutes or fractions of a minute late at the finish.

The attraction of score events lies in devising your circuit around the control points. You are trying to find a route that produces lots of points and doesn't retrace itself. Obviously the construction of this kind of course requires some thought at the start, and there are some basic rules that should be followed.

One advantage of score events is that a great number of competitors can be started in a small time – either a mass start or a series of mini-mass starts – without creating a procession. Not only are there probably a dozen ways of making a good circuit of the controls, but each circuit has a clockwise and an anticlockwise version.

As the high-scoring controls are usually on the periphery it is sensible to reach the border quickly and collect controls on the way. Sweep around the edges until time is running out and then come back in towards the finish, gathering more controls on the way. If the time has been misjudged it is good to have a few controls near at hand to fill in the time

Night events

The pleasures of night orienteering are only for the experienced performer, and until you are completely at home with navigation in broad daylight orienteering in the dark should be left to others.

Night events take place in rather easier terrain than is used for normal orienteering, and the controls are placed

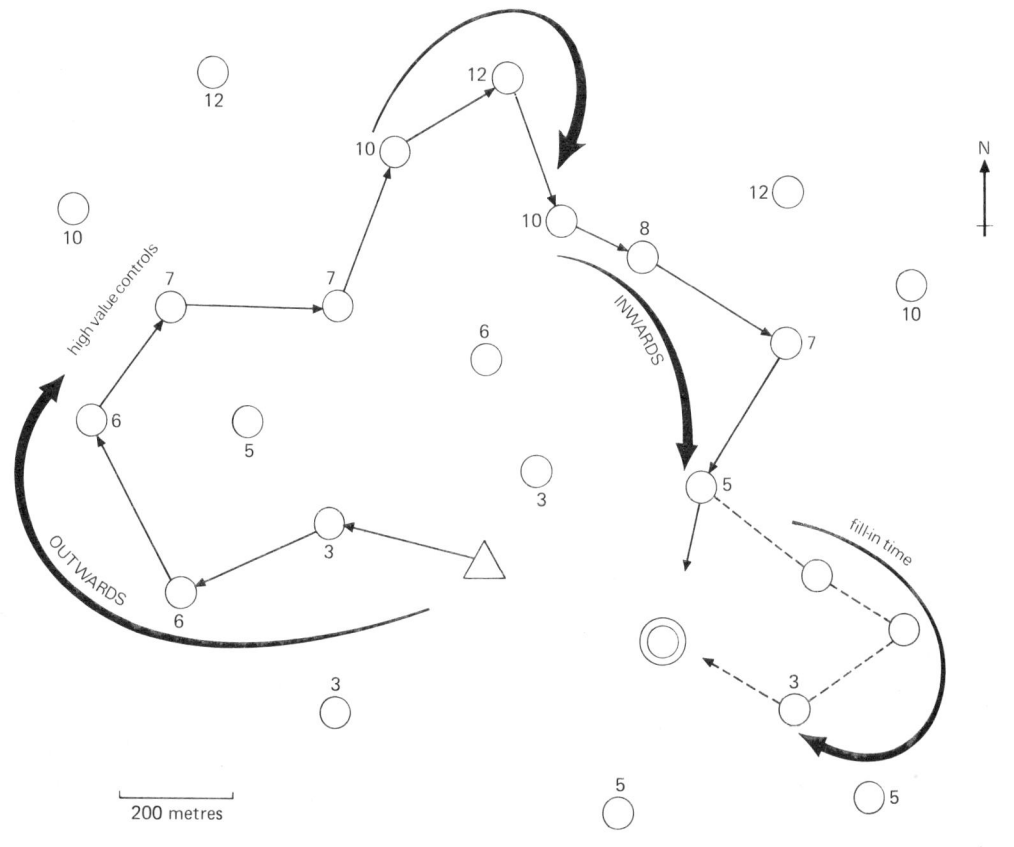

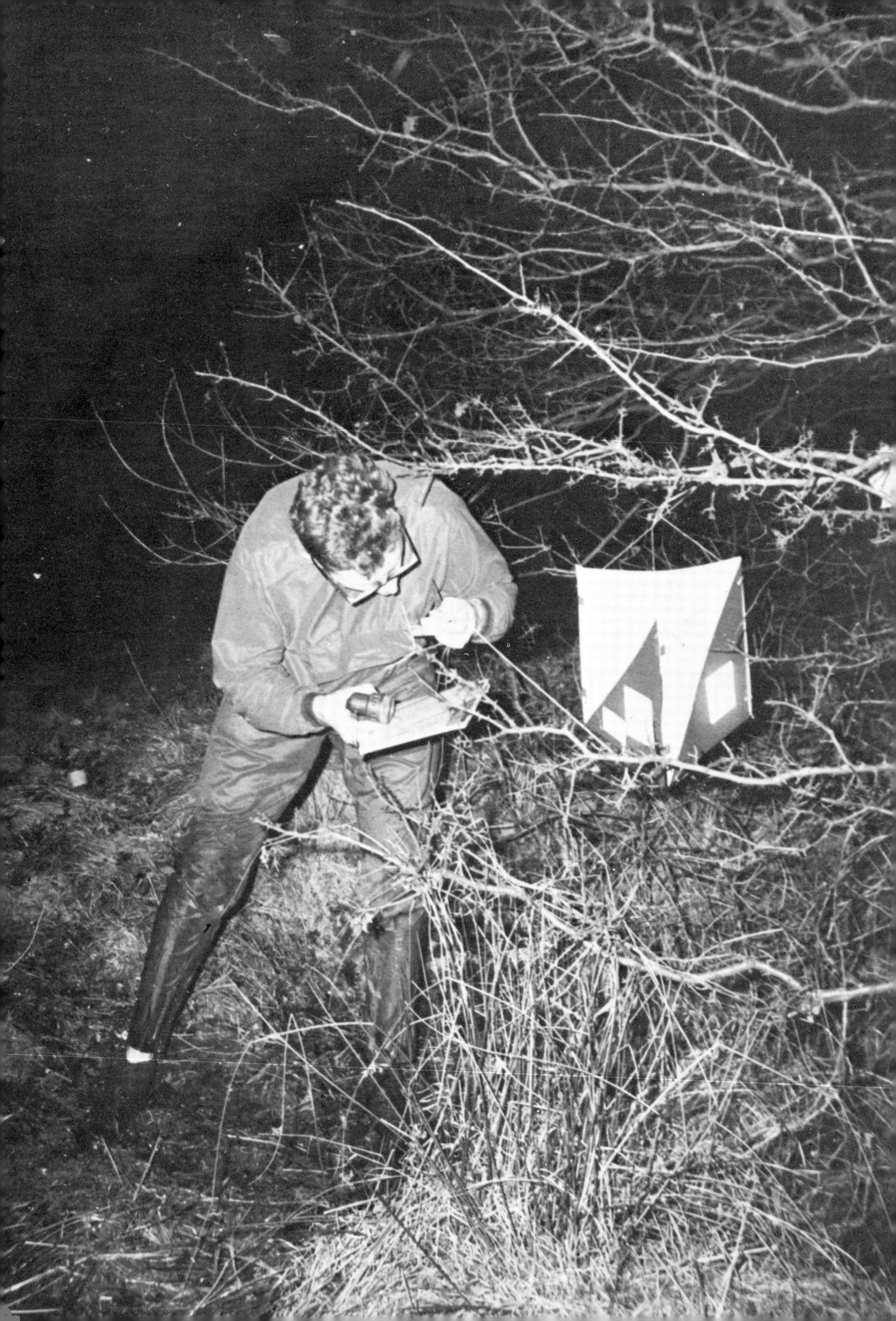

Left: *Darkness creates another dimension of difficulty by reducing the field of vision to the spread of a torch or head lamp.* Photo: John Disley

Right: *To encourage as little following as possible, relay courses are designed so that teams run over the same legs but in a different order. In this example there are three routes, but by switching the sequence at Control 4 an additional three variations can be made*

on more obvious features. Navigation at night relies much more on using good handrail and strong collecting features, for it is very difficult indeed to regain contact with the map when things go wrong in a pitch-black environment. Even with a good lamp your field of vision is reduced to 20 metres, and dark shadows make quite ordinary features look alien. In fact, one of the advantages of night events is that they can be held over areas that are too open and too well known for day use. Night orienteering has a charm of its own and no orienteer can say that he is fully experienced until he has completed a couple of these events.

You will need to add to the equipment described in Chapter 4 a good head lamp – obviously your hands will be full with map and compass, so a hand torch would be awkward, particularly when you want to take a bearing from the map. Your lamp needs to function at near full power for nearly two hours, and keen orienteers take along a spare torch, not to mention a spare bulb. They also ensure that the spare torch is plastic-bodied so as to reduce magnetic influence on the compass – the head lamp is far enough away not to have any effect on the needle.

Relays

These add another dimension to the normal stress of competition. Not only do you have the usual sense of personal urgency pushing you around the course as fast as possible, but a corporate responsibility for doing well. Some people respond magnificently to the added strain, while others go completely to pieces.

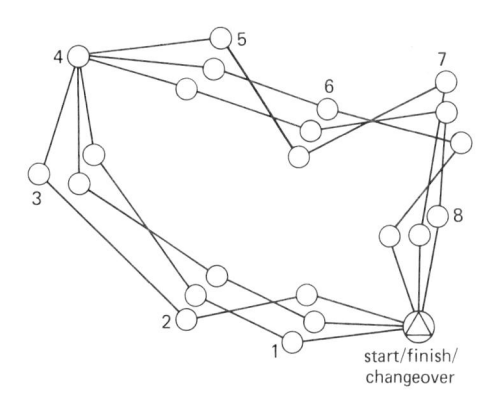

Relays provide excellent opportunities for practising self-control. A mass start is a time for practical assessment of your ability to be your own person: it's all too easy to follow the pack blindly as it streams away from the start. But who is leading it? Does he know where he's going? And if he does, is his destination necessarily yours? Some outstanding solo breakaways have been performed in relay races by first-leg runners who actually looked at the map before setting off, and resisted the temptation to rush lemming-like down the nearest forest track.

Relays are fun, and to avoid too much following, the pattern of courses is varied from team to team, so that although every team will actually run the same courses they will not necessarily do the circuits in the same order as other teams.

After you have joined a club you will have the opportunity to compete in several relays each year, and you will be able to select a course length much the same as you normally complete in individual competition. In fact, because of the problem of time and getting the competition finished before dark, relay courses are usually shorter than normal ones.

47

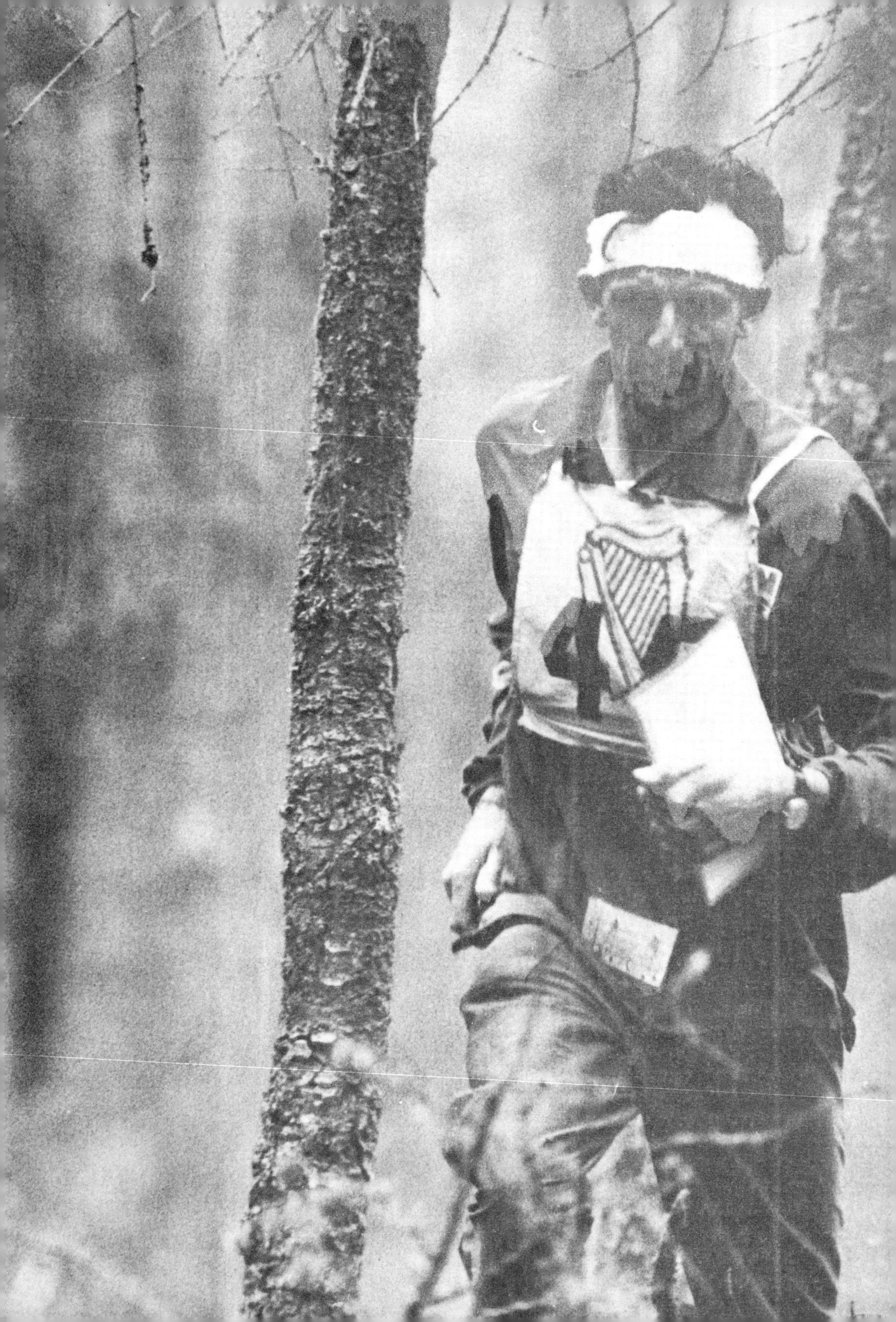

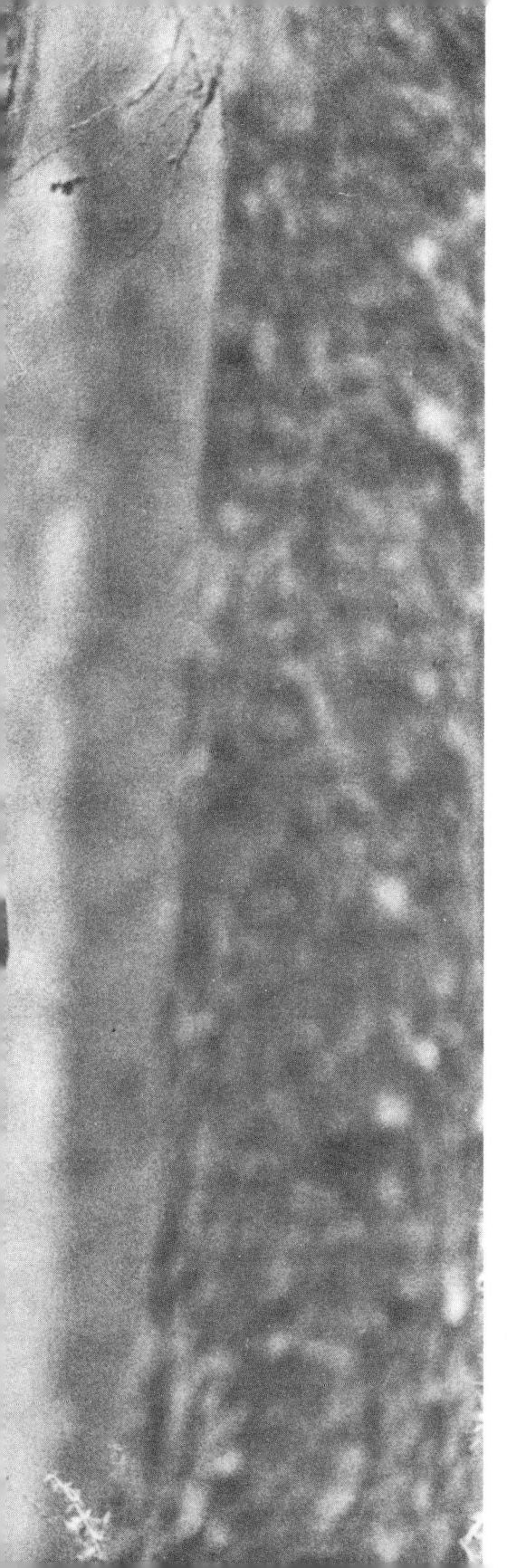

Chapter Four
Clothing, Equipment and Routines

Apart from a compass you probably already have enough suitable clothing and equipment to make a start at orienteering, as described in Chapter 1. There is no need to feel that you must have all the right gear for your first few sorties into the forest: orienteering clothing and equipment are extremely functional. In any case it is best to find out what you really need before spending money on colourful and interesting-looking equipment. Orienteering, like other sports, does have its specialist gear, and there is little doubt that once you become more enthusiastic you will want to help your performance by having the best equipment available. Suppliers' addresses are given in Appendix 1.

Footwear

The beginner should use the kind of footwear that is suitable for tramping through rough heathland. In summer this could mean a pair of trainers – jogging shoes with flat soles; in bad weather a pair of light boots or even wellingtons would give adequate protection. If you have a pair of studded football or hockey boots, these too are very suitable.

Later on, as you gain experience, you may feel that you should acquire some specialist footwear. Waterlogged boots or shoes are a handicap when you are trying to jog or run, particularly uphill;

A senior orienteer competing in a championship race. All the right accessories.
Photo: The Times

laces for wear before every race, and replace them before they break.

If you look after your shoes – and all the plastic variety needs is a wash – then even with regular use a pair should last for at least two years.

Clothing

For a start all garments should be expendable, as forests are rough and dirty places. The beginner will spend a considerable time standing still while working out which way to go next, so he or she might not be so warm as if taking a brisk country walk. Of course, once you are able to keep moving, more than enough heat can be generated. A pair of old blue jeans are as good as anything when starting orienteering. Above the waist a T-shirt with an old sweater or tracksuit blouse on top will be fine. If the weather is cold or wet, add an old anorak. A pull-on woollen cap might be worth taking if you expect to be out for a couple of hours on a cold day.

Whatever clothes you decide to wear, remember the BOF rule about all-over body cover, which means that you will have to wear long trousers, or breeches and long stockings, and long sleeves. This is because several years ago orienteers in Sweden ran the risk of contracting hepatitis, spread by blood from scratches and cuts infecting the washing facilities at events. Once overall body cover had been instigated the damage done by

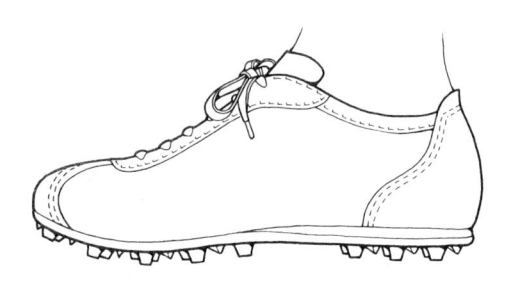

The keen orienteer needs a light, non-absorbent shoe that gives traction and support (a). For pre- and post-event activities a lightweight studded rubber boot (b) is very useful, particularly in muddy fields churned up by runners and cars

so are flat-soled shoes when the ground is wet and slippery. For the enthusiast the best orienteering shoe is the special lightweight kind made from very strong plastic fabric, with studs on the rubber sole. This shoe does not absorb water and its polished surface rejects mud, so that it stays light throughout the competition even after running through marshes and streams. The stud design on the sole gives excellent traction on slippery slopes and on vegetation-covered rocks. There are several different makes available, all good, and the best shoe is the one that fits your foot best.

Shoelaces on orienteering shoes are very vulnerable because the undergrowth rubs them through quickly. Check your

The O suit is a very functional garment designed to protect without impeding progress, and, when also wearing rubberized nylon stockings and non-absorbent underwear, the keen orienteer (a) remains lightweight even when soaking wet. The beginner and marginally competitive orienteer (b) can wear clothing usually associated with rambling – anorak, jersey and jeans

(a) (b)

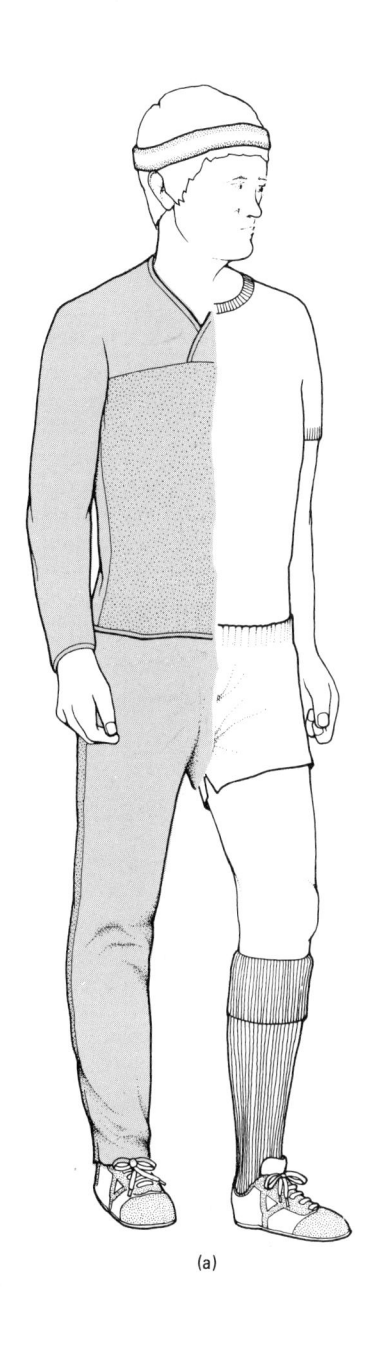

sharp foliage was drastically cut down, and the Swedes are now rid of the disease.

The keen, regular orienteer will wear an orienteering suit. These O suits are designed to give complete freedom of movement and protection without weight. They are made from breathing, lightweight knitted nylon, and although not waterproof they do keep out the wind and retain body heat in bad conditions surprisingly well. The smoothness of the material discourages snagging from brambles and thorns, as well as feeling pleasant next to the skin. The suits are loosely cut so that even when soaking wet they do not impede vigorous movement. Because of their thinness they dry quickly, so that an early shower in the woods can hardly be felt in the material by the end of the race. The O suit has a small pocket for whistle and pencil, secured by a strip of Velcro.

An alternative to trousers is a combination of nylon breeches and long stockings. A special type of stocking, called appropriately enough bramble-bashers, has a front panel of rubber; they are excellent value and are worn by most serious orienteers. Lightweight nylon gaiters are an alternative to bramble-bashers.

A headband, such as tennis players wear, is also very useful to stop sweat and rain getting in the eyes.

Underneath the O suit the experienced orienteer will probably wear just a pair of running shorts in the summer. In colder weather he will wear a long-sleeved vest and maybe even long-johns. The best underclothes are in man-made fibres, which will not absorb moisture, so that the garments stay dry and feel warm even after hard physical effort.

Compass

Even the best orienteers in the world, who can read a map in an instant, take a compass with them in competition. It is possible to get round an easy course, such as a wayfarers', without needing one, but for the serious competitor it is an essential piece of equipment.

The protractor-type compass developed by the Swedish Silva company is the only model suitable for orienteering. It is designed to perform at least four necessary functions for the orienteer, and is one of the best-designed pieces of equipment in any outdoor sports equipment shop. Even if you give up orienteering, the Silva compass will make rambling and fell-walking much more interesting as well as safer. Looked after carefully, it will be a friend for life.

The orienteering models, the Type 2NL and the Type 4S, incorporate special slide scales in the leading edge of the baseplate. The scales $1:10,000$; $1:20,000$; $1:25,000$; $1:50,000$; $1:15,000$ and $1:16,666$ correspond with the scales used for orienteering maps in Britain and abroad (see page 31). How to use the protractor compass will be dealt with in Chapter 5.

Whistle

For safety reasons BOF rules require all orienteers to carry a whistle when they compete, and a whistle check is often made in the pre-start area. In the unlikely event of a competitor being injured, the whistle is used to attract attraction and get help: the signal is six blasts followed by a minute's pause and then repeated. Carrying a light plastic whistle is no problem – it can go into a pocket fastened by a safety pin. Don't use a heavy metal police whistle, though: it will drive you mad jumping round in your pocket, and in any case might affect the magnetic needle in the compass.

Map case

A simple transparent cover for your map (usually about 180 × 260 millimetres) will make life much easier. A thin plastic bag will do to keep the map dry, but it is better to use a thicker-gauge plastic folder, like those used for filing documents. This will enable you to make a fairly flat surface on which to take a bearing when the map is folded. Orienteering shops sell for a few pence a good map case that is split into two compartments – a large one for the map and a smaller one for the control card. At championship events, where all competitors are pre-entered, the map will probably come already packaged in clear plastic; if so, the pre-race instructions will tell you.

Pen

A red ballpoint will do perfectly well to mark your map at the master maps, which are usually mounted on hardboard to give you a firm surface for copying. The only problem with a ballpoint is that it does not work well under water, and wet maps will not take biro marks. Keen orienteers have a second marker for wet days – a wax pencil such as a Chinagraph, which makes marks on wet paper and is also water-resistant, so that the marked course does not wash off halfway through the event. You will need some other coloured ballpoints too, if you are really keen – then you can make a professional job of your map corrections in, say, black, blue and green.

Very little specialist equipment is needed. The protractor compass (a) is perhaps the only item not already owned by the would-be orienteer; a purpose-made map case (b) is useful but can be improvised, and a digital watch (c) makes time checks easy

Spectacles

Many orienteers need to wear spectacles to read the map, and a piece of elastic joining the earpieces at the back of your head will prevent accidents. Incidentally, the cheapest National Health half-frame glasses are the best for orienteering, giving magnification where needed and allowing unobstructed vision for everything else.

Getting it all together

Carrying the bits and pieces can be quite a problem. The sooner you adopt an efficient system for placing all the various bits of paper, card, compass, whistle and pen, the sooner you will feel secure and confident.

The map, which will usually have to be folded, goes into the map case. The position of the fold may have to be left until you have drawn in your course at the master maps.

If the map case has a pocket for the control card, lodge this vital piece of equipment there. Otherwise it can go into the map case proper, back-to-back with the map.

Many orienteers like to keep the control card separate from the map case, so that they can punch the card without disturbing the map and possibly losing their place. They slide the card into its own plastic sleeve and pin it to the front of their O suit top with a big safety pin.

The control description sheet can be kept in the map case, but it is best to staple it to the face of the map on a section that is clearly superfluous to navigation. This is another job to add to the pre-race preparation list.

The whistle can be safety-pinned to the inside of your O suit pocket, and the red ballpoint, after it has done its job at the master maps, can join the whistle. The pocket can then be pressed shut with the Velcro strip.

That just leaves the compass, which can be held in the hand that isn't holding the map. Most compasses have a lanyard with a wrist loop which enables them to be instantly retrieved after your fingers have done some other task, like punching the control card or climbing a wall.

Finally, try and adopt a routine as well as a system both in the preparation period and during the race. If the minor actions can be made automatic, your mind can be kept free for more difficult problems like finding the way and ensuring that it is the best way.

Checklists

Before leaving home

1. Money for petrol, event fee, etc.
2. Road atlas, to find the event
3. Clothing and footwear:
   O suit, or jeans, shirt, jersey, anorak
   T-shirt, shorts
   Bramble-bashers or stockings
   Headband
   Shoes – studs, boots
4. Equipment:
   Compass
   Whistle
   Map case
   Pens
   Safety pins
   Stapler
   Spectacles (if worn)
5. Post-event wear:
   Warm clothes – wellingtons for wet fields
   Towel
   Plastic carrier bag for wet gear
   Umbrella
6. Sustenance:
   Packed lunch
   Thermos flask of tea/coffee/soup
   Soft drinks
7. First aid:
   Antiseptic and plasters for cuts and grazes

Leaving for the start

1. Properly dressed – all-over body cover?
2. Whistle
3. Compass – with correct scale if Silva Type 4S or 2
4. Map (if distributed at registration) – corrected?
5. Map case (if there isn't an official case)
6. Control card, in map case or pinned to shirt in plastic case – appropriately filled in on both sections?
7. Control description sheet – in map case or stapled to front of map
8. Red ballpoint or Chinagraph pencil – if master maps
9. Red tape arrow on thumb (see Chapter 6)
10. Spectacles – cleaned?

Before leaving the event

1. Is your control card with the finish officials?
2. Is your finish time hung up, if it is a self-help system?
3. Collect details of forthcoming events if not already stuck under your windscreen wipers.
4. Check that nothing has been left behind, including muddy shoes and stockings left on the grass when you changed.
5. If you enjoyed the event, try and find someone to thank. It will probably make their day.

Back at home

1. Wash and clean gear.
2. Study your map and draw in your route.
3. Write comments on the reverse that will be helpful in the future.
4. Start a file of your O maps and results.

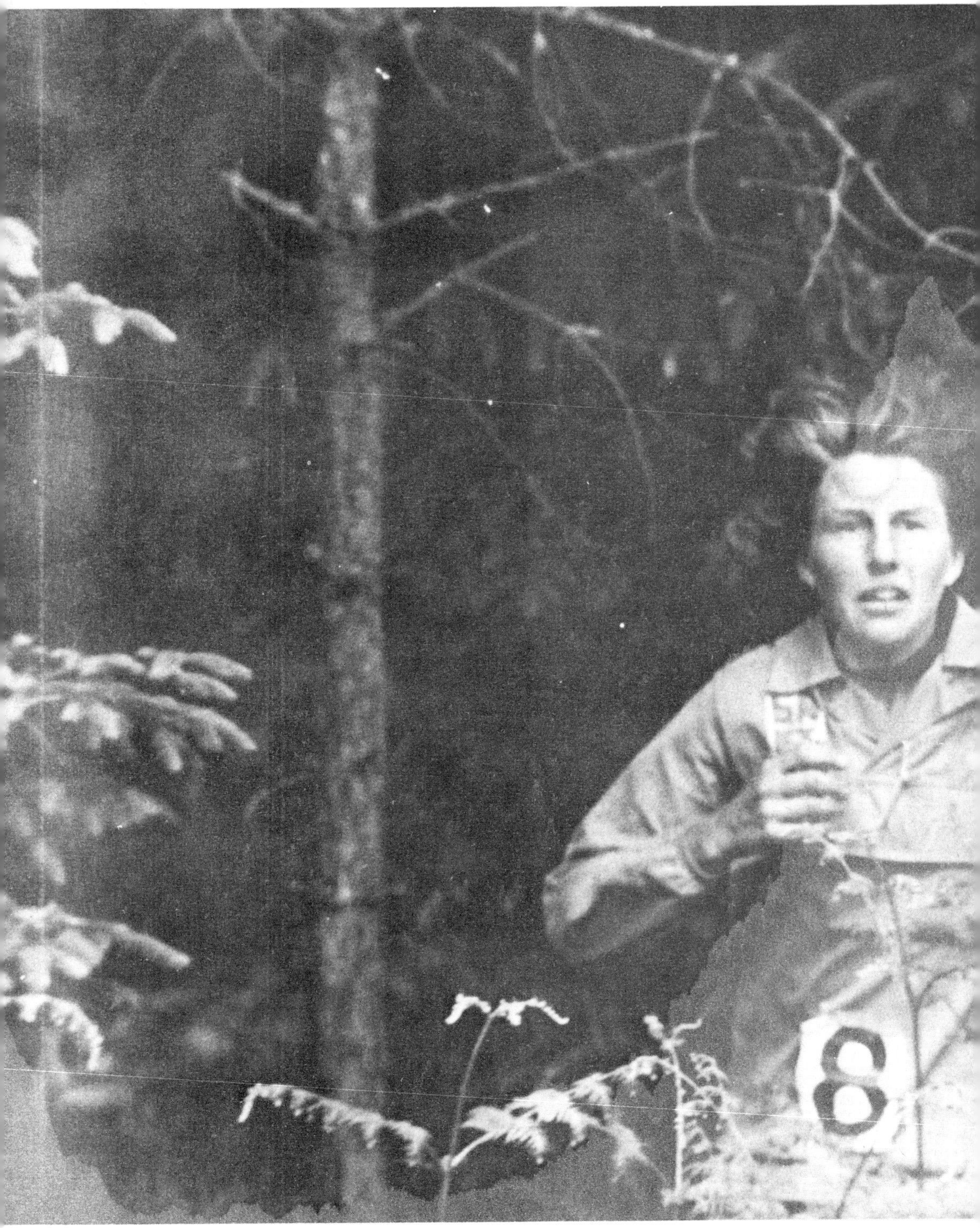

Chapter Five
Using the Compass

There are several fundamental wayfaring techniques which all orienteers apply to those stock situations which occur during an event. They are the kind of methods which all navigators use almost instinctively whether they are exploring unknown country or sailing single-handed round the world. Some of these techniques use a compass to determine direction.

The orienteering compass

The only practical compass for the orienteer, as explained in Chapter 4, is the protractor type, which not only provides information on the direction of magnetic north, but can also be used both as a protractor to find bearings from the map, and as a sighting compass for taking bearings in the terrain. Additionally, it provides a straight edge which can be used as a scale to determine distance, and a magnifying lens to enlarge the details on finely drawn maps.

The various parts

The compass needle, balanced to swing evenly for the part of the world where it is going to be used, rotates on a sapphire bearing inside a transparent

---

A great sense of urgency combined with intense concentration drives this elite orienteer through the forest. Photo: The Times

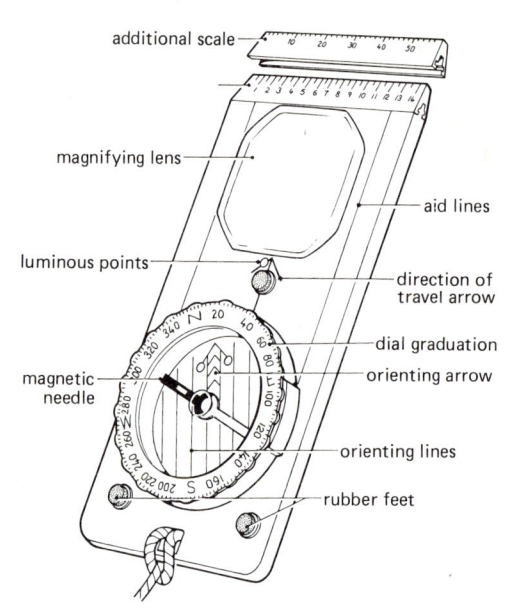

The protractor compass is a perfect instrument designed to do a particular job with accuracy and without complication. It is vital for any orienteer who wants to be competitive

capsule. The capsule is filled with anti-static liquid, which ensures that the free-swinging needle settles accurately and quickly, an important factor when seconds are vital; a steady needle is also valuable when using a compass on the move. The capsule has parallel orienting lines engraved on its under-surface. It is set in either plastic or alloy, and is marked with the normal direction points, NESW, and the 360 degrees. The housing turns freely but firmly, to avoid accidental movement, on a strong, transparent plastic baseplate which carries various markings that are helpful when taking bearings and measuring distances on the map. Most models, as mentioned above, also have a lens.

A direction bearing from the O map

This is the bread-and-butter technique of map and compass work, and really it is very simple. There is nothing difficult about understanding bearings: a bearing is just another name for an angle. Very conveniently orienteering maps are drawn to magnetic north, so that there is no need to make any corrections to match map bearings with compass bearings.

1. Place the compass on the map so that the long edge of the baseplate joins together your present position with your destination. Check that the direction-of-travel arrow is pointing towards your destination.

On the orienteering map degrees are measured clockwise from the north–south lines. In the forest the same direction is found by counting degrees from the direction pointed out by the red end of the compass needle

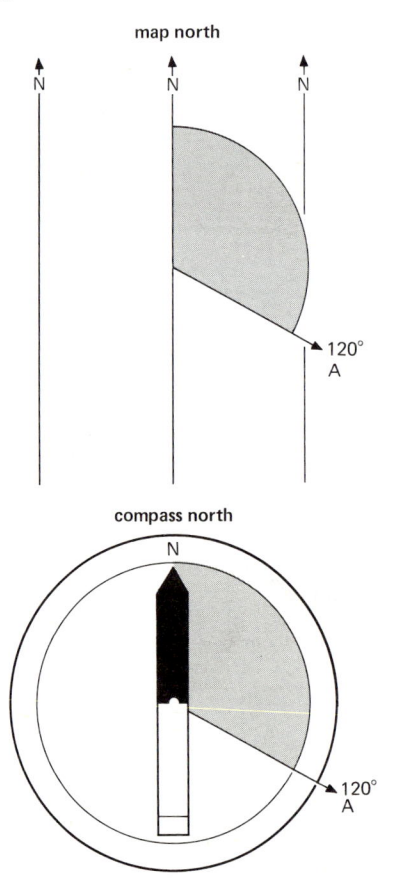

(a)

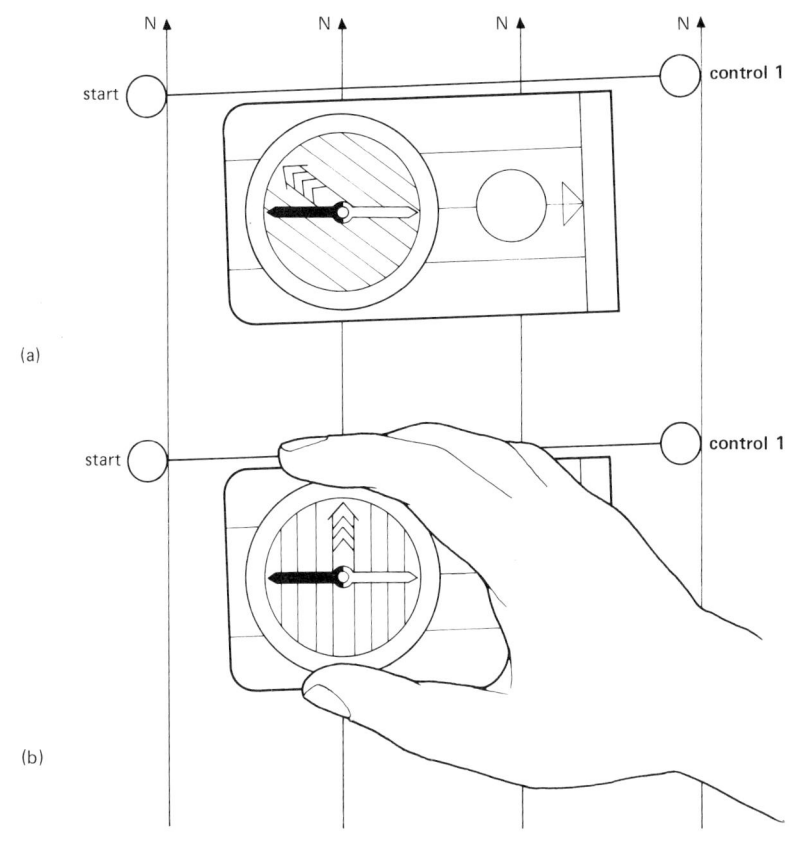

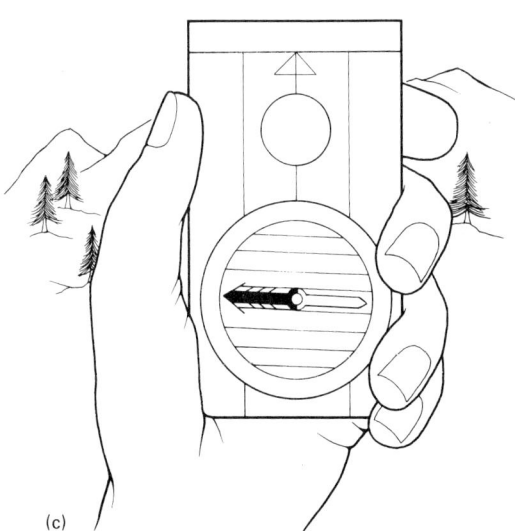

(b)

(c)

Taking bearings in three simple stages, as described in the text

2. Keep the baseplate firm on the map and turn the compass housing until the orienting lines are parallel to the north-south lines on the map. Then check that the orienting arrow is pointing to north on the map.

3. Lift the compass off the map. Hold it horizontal by the short end so that it sticks out in front of your waist. Turn yourself and the compass until the red end of the needle points to the north mark on the housing dial. Look up over the compass and you will be facing the feature you wanted to locate.

Note that in steps 1 and 2 the compass needle can be totally ignored. You should practise this technique at home on any map until it requires no thought. You will have enough to think about in the forest without trying to remember how to take a bearing.

Setting a map

The quickest way to set a map is to align the map with linear features such as a track or boundary that are visible on the ground. However, there are many times when no convenient major objects can be seen, and then a compass can easily be used.

1. Place the compass anywhere on the map.

2. Turn the map and compass as one unit until the red end of the needle points to north on the map.

The map is now set. Take the compass off, and the features in the terrain should match up with the appropriate marks on the map.

As you become more experienced you will keep the map set at all times, always progressing over map and country with thumb and feet in harmony.

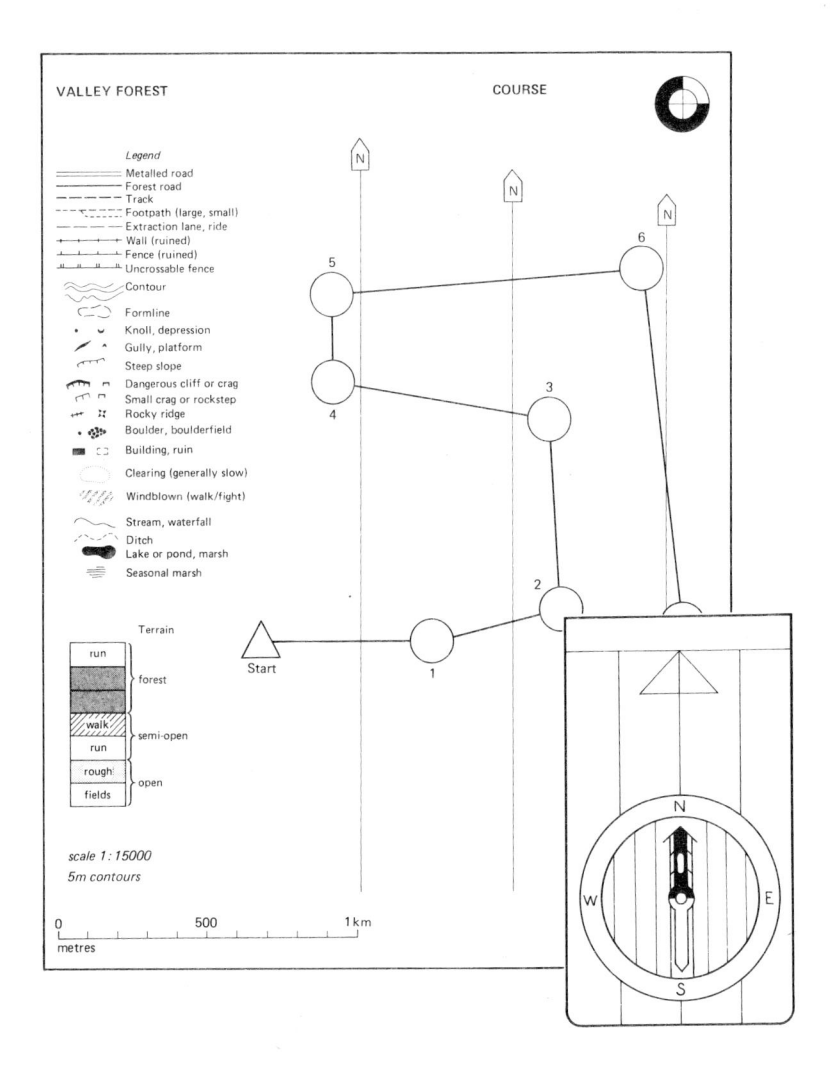

Setting a map – the second stage as described in the text above

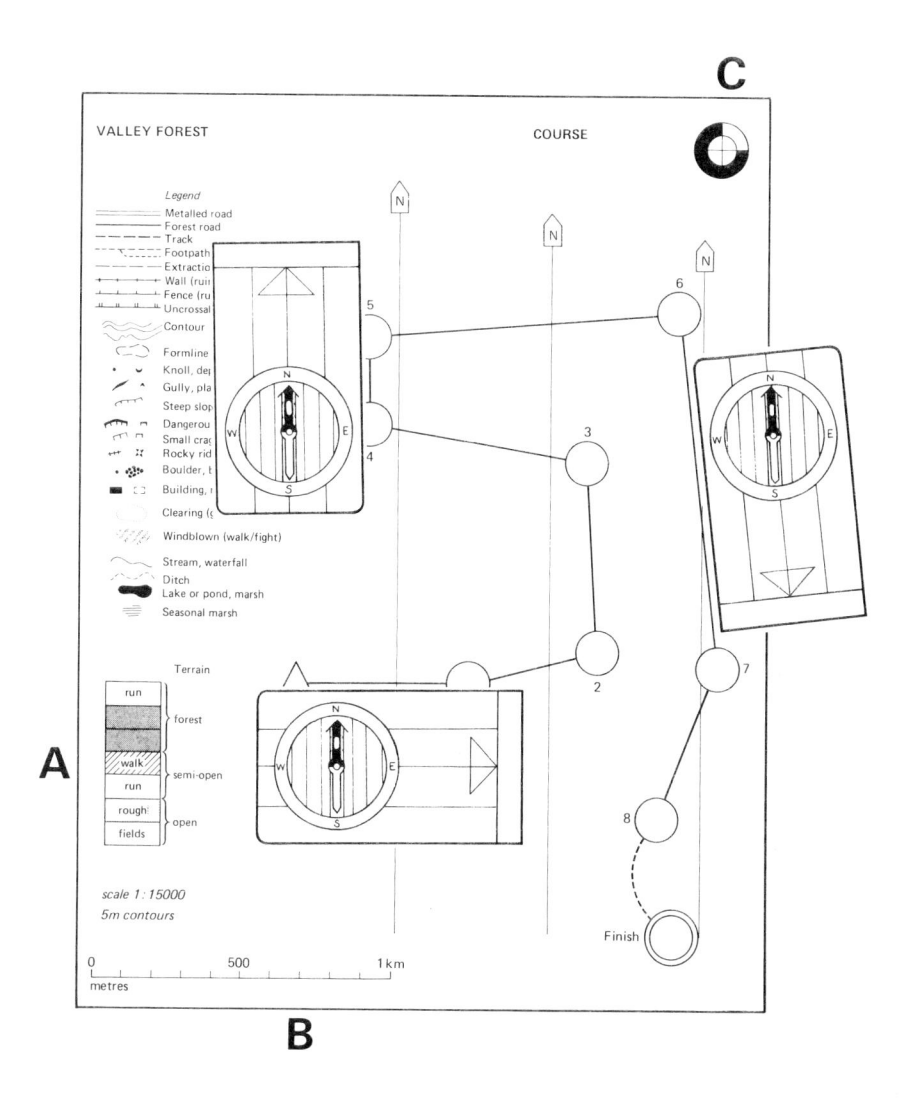

The map should remain in a set position all round the course, so that features on the ground match up to their representations on the map at all times. In this diagram the orienteer will be behind the short edge of the compass after every change of direction, e.g. at point A when going to Control 1, at BG when going to Control 5, and at C when coming south to Control 7. In fact the map, once set, remains fixed in relation to the heavens, while the orienteer rotates around its edges as he changes direction

61

Taking a bearing on the ground

It is often necessary to work backwards from the terrain to the map, particularly when temporarily lost, but able to see an identifiable feature in the distance. A bearing on this feature can then be used to locate your position on the map – as long as you are on a linear feature.

    1. Point the baseplate at the feature, with the direction-of-travel arrow pointing away from you.

    2. Keep the baseplate steady and turn the housing until the north mark on the dial is opposite the red end of the needle.

    3. Place the compass on the map with the long edge touching the feature you have just used to take a bearing. Pivot the baseplate around this point until the orienting lines in the capsule are parallel with the north–south lines on the map. Check that the orienting arrow is pointing to north on the map.

It is very helpful to be able to use a bearing taken on a recognizable feature to plot your position on the map. See text for instructions

    4. Your position is now somewhere along the line made by the edge of the compass. If you are on a track, then your exact position is where the edge cuts the track on the map.

Accurate travel on a bearing

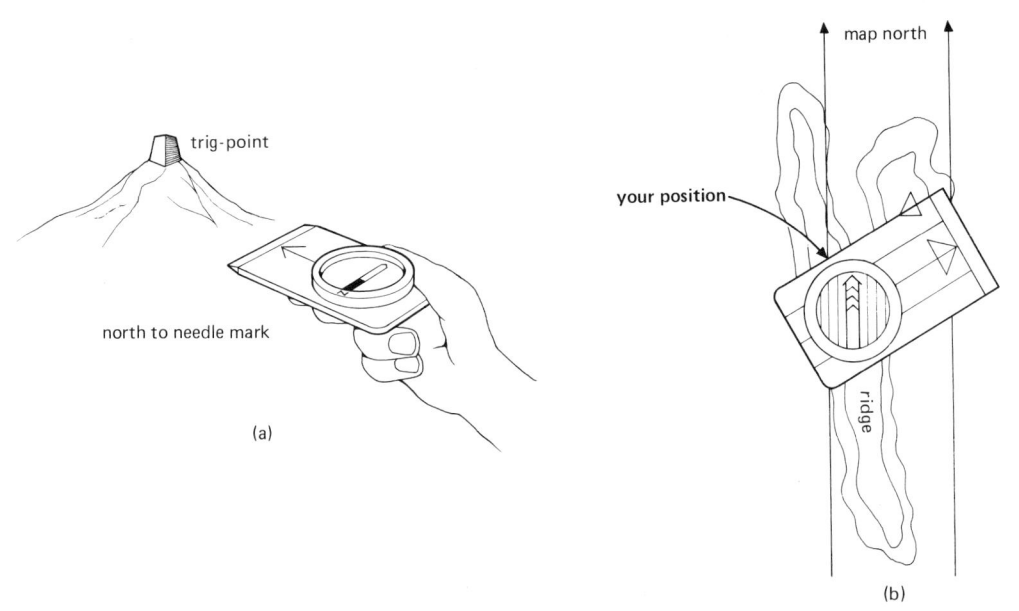

With practice it is possible to sight a protractor-type Silva compass on a bearing to an accuracy of a couple of degrees, but to achieve this accuracy you must give the compass needle every chance of settling properly. First, storage: keep your compass away from other magnetic influences; don't store it in a drawer with other metal objects like scissors; don't carry it about in an anorak pocket with a clasp knife; keep it away from the speaker in your car radio. Second, make sure that the compass needle swings freely when you take a bearing. Keep the baseplate horizontal. See that there are no external influences affecting the needle. Is your watch or watchstrap ferrous? What about the zip on your anorak? Are you leaning on an iron gate or up against a wire fence? Significant errors can be produced by such things.

Having taken the bearing:

1. Sight over the baseplate and pick out a feature about 50–100 metres away that is dead on line. Make sure that the feature you select is distinctive enough for you to recognize it again after looking away.

2. Stop looking at the compass and walk, jog or run to your target. It isn't necessary to travel on a precise line to your destination, and you can side-step to avoid obstacles such as fallen trees, bramble patches and small marshes. You just want the quickest way to your objective.

3. Arrive at your feature and then repeat the exercise until you reach your final destination.

This method of travel isn't particularly quick, especially in poor visibility which may mean that each leg of a sighting will be only 25–30 metres, but it is an accurate way of crossing the terrain and can be used to find small features from a point up to about 200 metres away.

Rough travel on a bearing

It is quite common to find that only a rough assessment of direction is required on some parts of the course, for instance when you are aiming at a broad collecting feature. This doesn't mean that your initial bearings from the map should be rough, but rather that your course through the forest need not be precise. All you need do is check with the compass every 50 metres or so that you are still heading in the right direction. With practice you will find that you can run with the compass held steady in front of you for a few seconds just to give the needle a chance to settle, and then you can glance down and see what is happening. If the needle isn't pointing at the north mark on the capsule housing, you have swerved off course. The experienced orienteer can over-correct his next leg and keep remarkably straight through the terrain without pausing.

Coarse compass travel

When no more than approximate direction is needed, it is only necessary to use the compass needle as a guide. For instance, when the next collecting feature is due north of your present position, just run in the direction in which the red end of the needle points. If the direction is due west, keep the needle pointing past your right shoulder. This technique saves those few seconds needed to take a bearing properly from the map, seconds which are important to a keen racer.

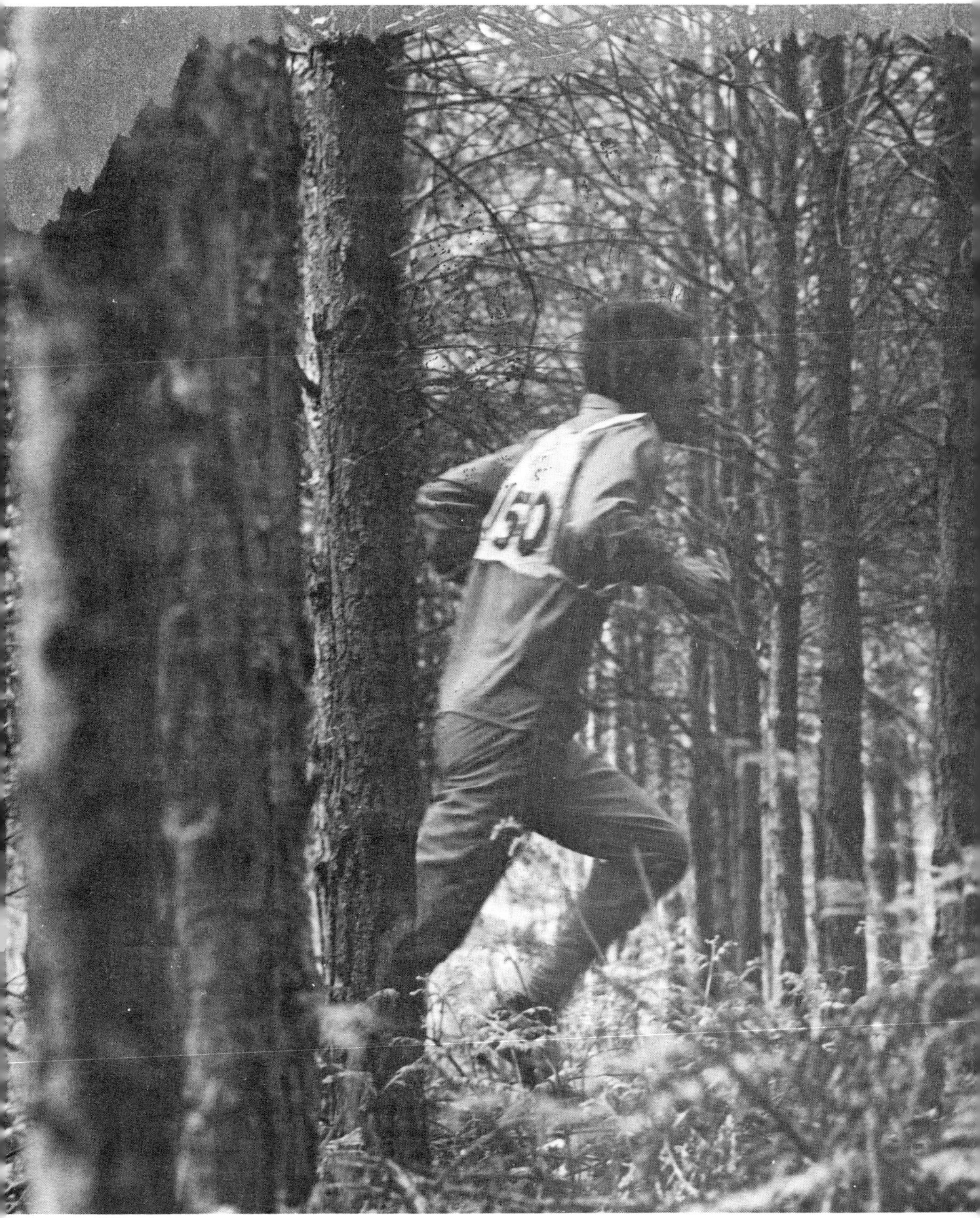
50

Chapter Six
Basic Orienteering Techniques

The twin components of navigation are direction and distance, and we have already seen in Chapter 5 that direction is not too difficult to find, either with precise compass work or on coarse needle travel. More orienteering mistakes are made by misjudging distance than from any other cause. The reason is that the forest is always changing its surface and its intervisibility. Most orienteers can estimate 100 metres ahead when looking down a straight forest road – motorway turn-off markers give good visual practice at estimating 100-metre sections. But it is a different story when the 100 metres is in the forest and over broken terrain: then it is a case of trying to add a succession of disjointed vistas to complete the required distance. In situations like this it is essential to estimate distance by every possible means.

Estimating distance

Checking off features on the map and ground

When crossing a well-detailed area on the map it is possible to progress from point to point by ticking off prominent features as you pass them. It is very easy when running on a bearing to switch off mentally and miss vital clues which are recording your progress. Obviously line features such as streams, tracks and

The open forest provides good running but with visibility reduced to thirty seconds' worth of activity. Photo: John Cleare

1. stream ....✓
2. fence ....✓
3. path ....✓
4. track ...
5. ridge ...
control ...

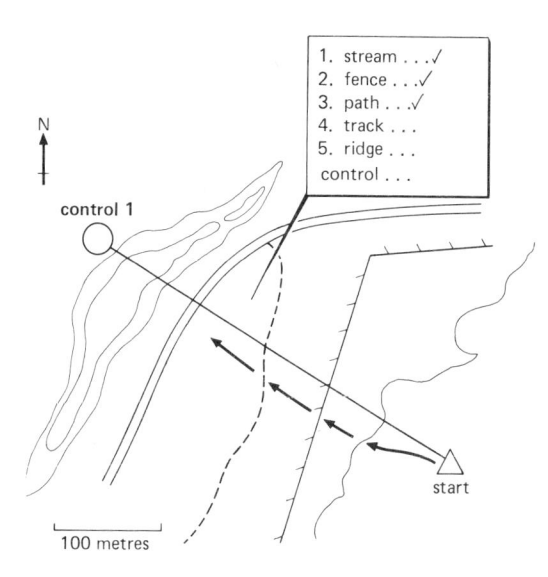

Progress across the map towards the control can be checked by ticking off prominent features as they are passed. Linear features like streams, fences and tracks are obviously the easiest to recognize and the hardest to miss

boundaries that cross your route are the best indicators of distance, but when you are on a line feature you will need to note various point features that punctuate your progress, for instance vegetation changes, fence corners, and junctions with tracks, paths and streams.

The ability to memorize forthcoming features after a brief look at the map will be well rewarded by a continuous run without time-wasting stops to correlate the map with every fresh feature reached. As in chess, the good orienteer is thinking several moves ahead, rather than playing each feature on its own.

Step counting

It is always wise to double-check as much as possible the evidence elicited from the map. There is always a chance that new features have appeared overnight – for instance, just one gang of men cutting timber on contract for forty-eight hours in the forest can create several additional tracks and clearings. And there is always the chance that you are not exactly on the line you think you are, and indulging in the classic exercise of bending the map to match the ground.

A good way of checking is by step counting from one reliable feature to the next positively identified point, so if you meet an orienteer in a lonely part of the forest and find him reluctant to do more than nod his head in reply to your greeting, the chances are that he is busy counting steps.

The technique involves counting alternate footfalls – in other words, every time your left foot hits the ground you count. You will need to work out your own step count figure, but generally 100 metres is used as a base for calculations. Measure out 100 metres over some rough but reasonably flat grassland; this can be done by walking with long strides – 100 of them – and putting down markers at either end of the stretch. Then run or jog over this distance at your normal speed during an event – count the double steps as described above. You should have a figure between 33 and 50, depending on your length of leg and your pace. Repeat the exercise several times in both directions and then average out the figures. You can now make this figure your norm for travelling over level, reasonably rough going. If it is 39, you can expect to reduce this figure when running on a good track or path, perhaps to 35. If your good track is uphill you will be back up to your norm of 39 again or even higher. In really rough terrain, where you have to jump over cut brashings or push through thigh-high bracken, your norm-plus figure may be up to 50.

Only experience will give you the correct ratios for your step count over varied ground and on different gradients, but once you have a trustworthy bracket of figures you can move confidently across featureless terrain and still, by step counting carefully, have a very good idea of how far you have travelled from the last known feature.

Measuring distance on the map

Now that you have a step count figure, you will need a quick and accurate way of measuring distance on the map. With practice it is possible to judge with some accuracy 1 centimetre on the map. Then, depending on the scale, 1 centimetre can be converted to a distance on the ground; for instance, with the 1:10,000 scale, by crossing off the last two zeros we get 100 metres for 1 centimetre. This method has already been mentioned in Chapter 2.

If you are good at mental arithmetic you would be able to convert 3.7 centimetres on the map to metres on the ground at a scale of 1:15,000 in the proverbial twinkling of an eye (555 metres). However, the real question is can you estimate distance with the eye and still do the sums when you are running uphill, with other things on your mind? Most of us can't, so we simplify matters, and contrive to measure 100-metre units accurately on the map by fixing a scale to the front edge of our compass. Our eye can judge 1 centimetre, but is fallible for longer sections.

The most convenient device is the changeable plastic scale fitted to the front edge of the Silva Type 4S and Type 2 compasses. The small slides are engraved to cover six different map scales, so make sure that you have the correct slide fitted to your compass for the map you receive at registration; if the maps are only given out at the start, the information about scale will have

These sets of step scales are for 36/37, 42/43 and 49/51 step counts to the 100 metres, as applied to 1:15,000 and 1:20,000 scale maps. Such scales can be stuck to the leading edge of the compass baseplate

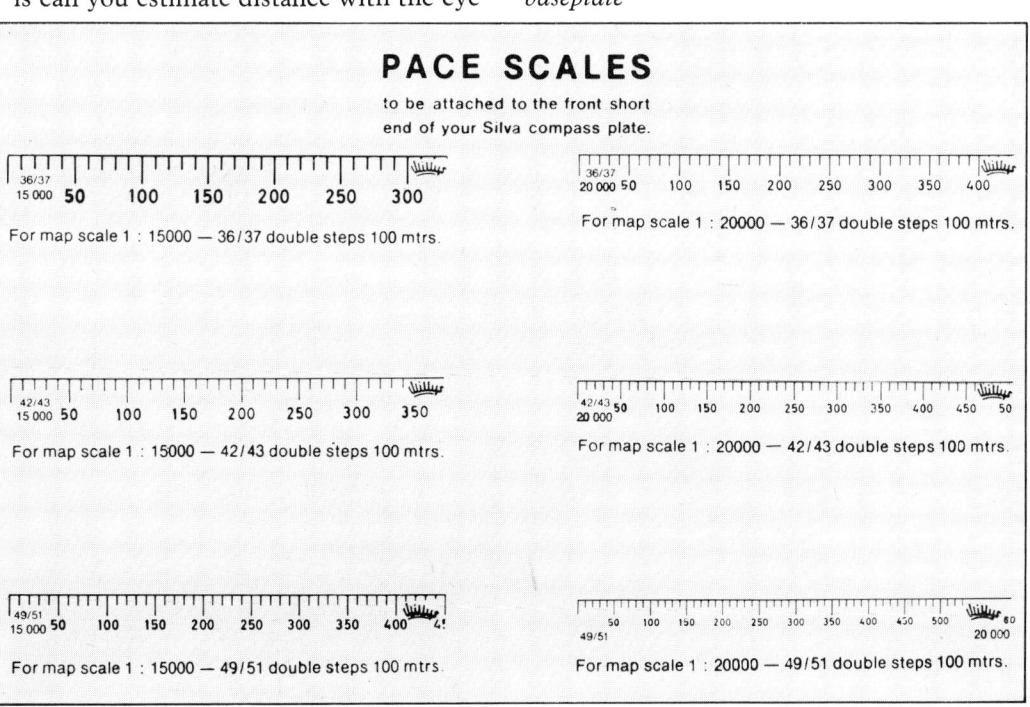

PACE SCALES
to be attached to the front short end of your Silva compass plate.

For map scale 1 : 15000 — 36/37 double steps 100 mtrs.

For map scale 1 : 20000 — 36/37 double steps 100 mtrs.

For map scale 1 : 15000 — 42/43 double steps 100 mtrs.

For map scale 1 : 20000 — 42/43 double steps 100 mtrs.

For map scale 1 : 15000 — 49/51 double steps 100 mtrs.

For map scale 1 : 20000 — 49/51 double steps 100 mtrs.

appeared in the organizer's pre-event literature.

It is possible to convert an ordinary compass by making your own scales and sticking them on the compass with transparent adhesive tape. You will find that most maps have a visual scale printed on them which clearly shows 100-metre sections. This scale can be copied or cut out and stuck on the compass. The obvious disadvantages of the stick-on scale are that it wears badly and needs frequent replacing, and that, perversely, next week's map is always a different scale from last week's.

This method of measuring 100-metre units still leaves the orienteer with some simple multiplication to do while on the move (multiplying his personal step count figure), but as it is seldom necessary to measure any distance further than 300 or 400 metres, the multiplication is never too complicated.

However, the maths can be eliminated totally by making a scale that measures your step count figures. With care and a calculator, a scale can be constructed that will indicate ten-step intervals. To construct your own step scale see Appendix 3. It will make life easier if these scales are stuck on to the slides of your compass, so that you are not constantly peeling off your handiwork to cope with a fresh map scale.

Like compass work, step counting is a back-up technique to map-reading. It will certainly be invaluable in terrain without prominent features, but always remember that reading the map is the simplest and quickest way of navigating.

The first control

Even the most experienced orienteers do not feel relaxed until they have tuned themselves in to the map, and established

Playing themselves in carefully, competitors use a forestry road to make their way towards the first control.

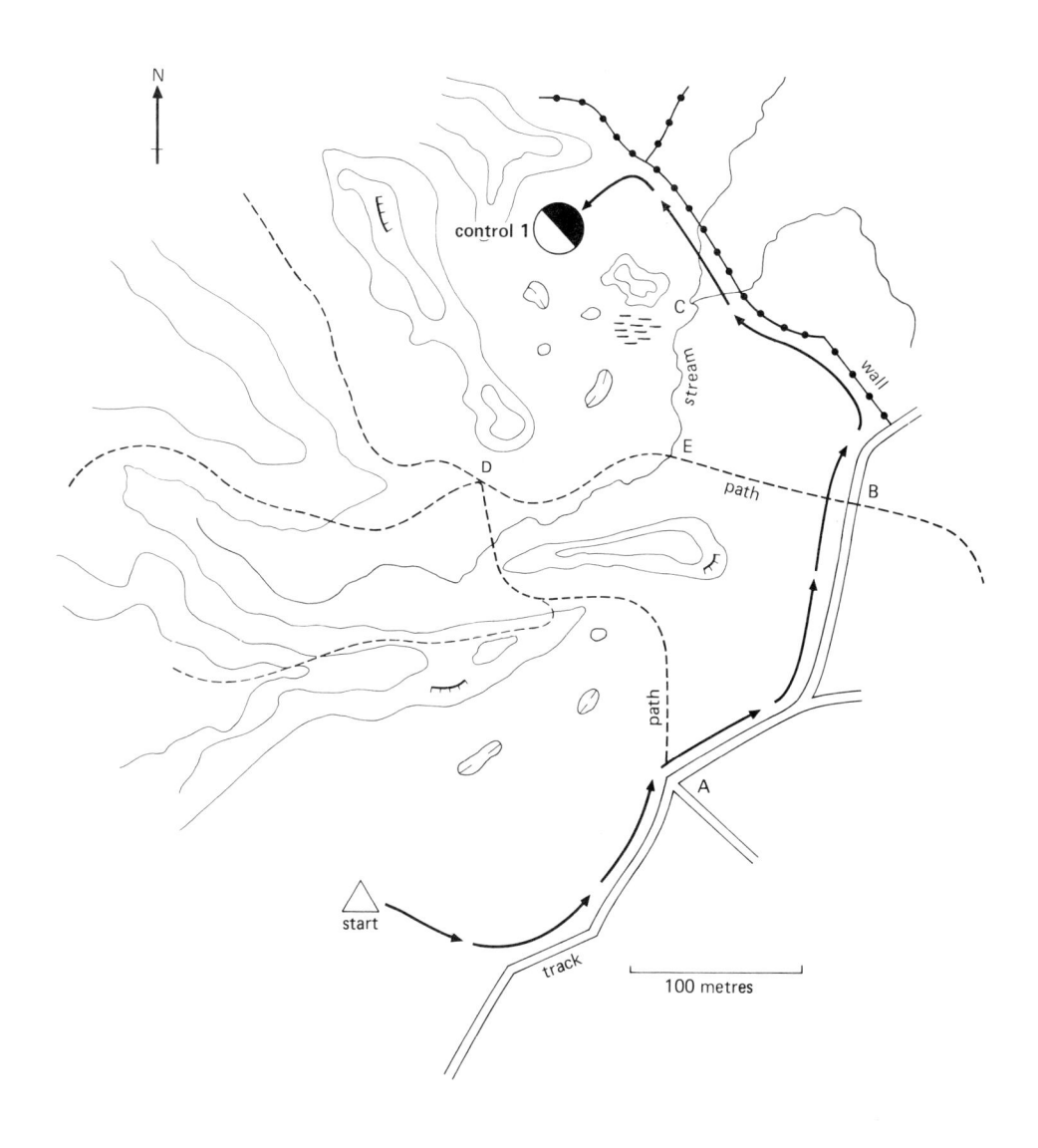

It is always safer, even for old-stagers, to play yourself in on a new map in unfamiliar terrain. The route above uses handrails – the track and the wall – to reach an attack point within 75 metres of the control. During this safe run the orienteer can note how various features are dealt with by the mapmaker. The same leg met later in a race would probably be taken direct through point D, or the path turn-offs at A or B would be used to shorten the route. The attack point at the stream junction C would also be used in preference to the wall junction round the back of the control

their exact position on it. At the start or at the master maps all the competitors are still in the hands of the course designer – like a puppet master, he has led them on strings to a position in the forest which he has marked on the map with a red triangle. It is vital that as soon as the strings are cut the orienteer takes the initiative and locates himself to his own satisfaction on the map and ground.

Usually this will mean finding a major feature such as a track, field corner or boundary junction. World championship calibre orienteers will devise such a route to Control 1 rather than risk a cross-country route at this stage of the race. A few extra metres run on a detour are considered very worthwhile if they put the orienteer in touch with the map.

For the beginner it is foolish to strike out across difficult terrain from the start. Always try and find a path and track system that will take you towards the control, and then when the jigsaw starts to fit together, with map and ground in harmony, you can confidently enter the real forest between the line features.

Paths or cross-country?

Route choice is one of the most intriguing aspects of navigation, and the most frequent choice offered to the orienteer is between going from point to point by paths and tracks, or taking a direct route through the natural forest.

Path running has two advantages: first, the actual surface is runnable; and second, a path is a handrail (see below), which allows a certain relaxation of effort, or, more constructively, gives the orienteer time to work out, while on the move, the logistics of the next section of the course. Certainly for a beginner path following is the best way of ensuring that an event is completed without too much drama; in other words the course

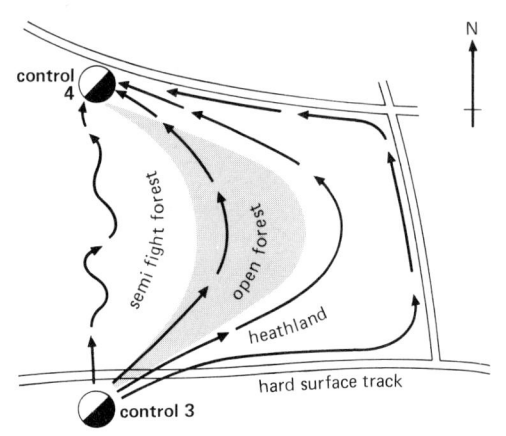

Whether to run further on a good path or take short cuts and risk tough conditions is always a hard choice. Only experience will provide a formula for your own personal strengths and weaknesses

should be taken as a succession of first controls.

With some experience the merits of cutting off corners and making direct routes through the trees will encourage the newcomer to seek alternatives to paths. Only by practice and careful observation will it be possible to work out how to relate path distance to virgin forest distance. The path route can be three times as long as the forest one, particularly if navigation checks are necessary on the direct route.

British orienteering takes place in forests that are more overlaid by the hand of man than are Scandinavian forests, where orienteering began, but despite the problems of too many paths and tracks the British course planner does try and make a course that rewards forest running. As you get better you will find that route choice is slightly loaded on the side of free running in the open forest, and that is the joy of the sport.

Around or over?

Running uphill is hard work; in fact even walking up steep slopes isn't easy,

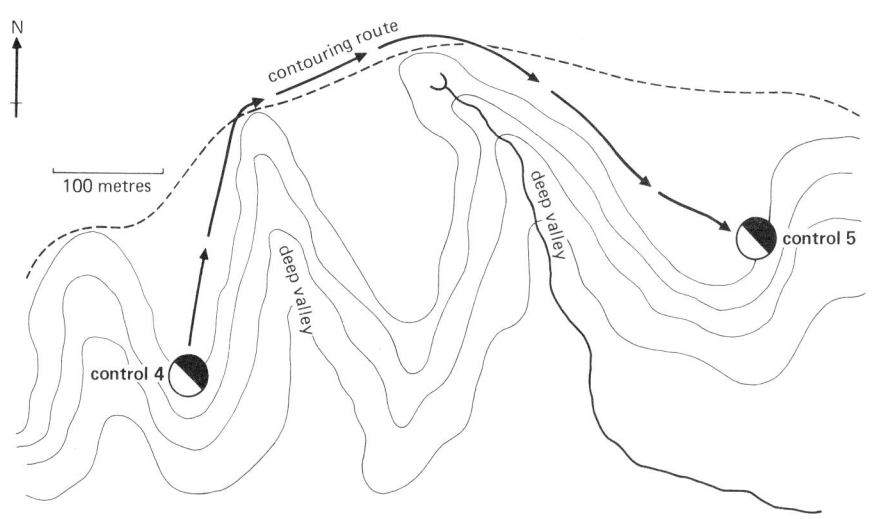

Generally you should try to avoid losing height in situations where it has to be regained. Look for a way above or below any system of ridges and valleys that lie between you and the next control. The contouring route will often pick up a path as a bonus

particularly when you are starting to feel weary. Consequently the orienteer looks very carefully at any route that climbs up over several contours. Obviously if the next control is 80 metres higher than your present elevation, all you can do is grit your teeth and press on. What orienteers are anxious to avoid is unnecessary height loss – up and down, or down and up, on the way from one point to another. Course planners love to include sections that cross the grain of the country, so contouring around the crest of a deep valley or following the hem around the bottom of a ridge are always worth considering as a quicker and less energy-sapping alternative to a brutal frontal attack straight up a hill. It always pays to count contours, particularly in situations as shown below, which arise frequently in hilly terrain.

Handrails

Intelligent navigation makes use of linear features wherever possible. Tracks, paths, boundaries, power lines, ridges, railways, valleys and streams are all examples of linear features; they can lead the orienteer by the hand (or at any rate the foot) across the terrain with certainty and ease, for not only do handrails offer direction, but they also provide natural pathways. Even if the handrails are not actual paths or tracks, linear features often give better going by their side than does the adjacent forest. The vegetation isn't so thick, visibility is better, and animals have often made minor paths in

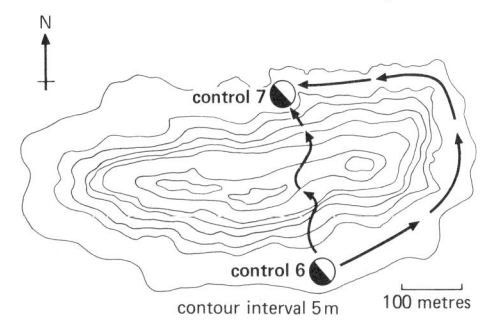

Only experience will give you a formula for height versus distance, but as a general rule two contour intervals (10 metres) equal 100 metres on the flat. One point often overlooked is that steep slopes can be as difficult to come down as to climb up

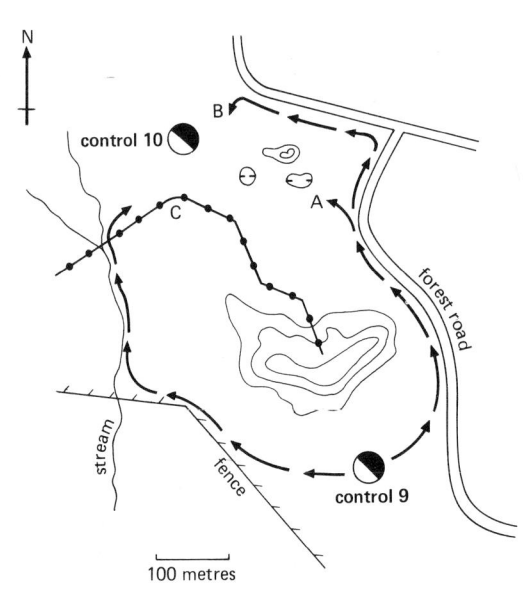

off to one side of his target, and then, having run far enough, turns inwards to find the control.

This technique works best when the control is on a collecting feature – a linear feature that lies across the orienteer's path as he approaches. It doesn't much matter which way you aim off, and about 50 metres over a section of 300 metres should be ample. It is better actually to take a bearing on a point 50 metres to one side of the control circle and then run on rough compass technique. Although aiming off adds metres to your route, it does pay dividends in time saved.

The obvious handrail from Controls 9 to 10 is the forestry road to the east. It can be used right through to the corner at point B, or just as far as A if the orienteer thinks he can use the small features to navigate from there to the control. The route to the west uses three handrail – the fence, the stream and the wall. Although the going won't be as fast as the track, it will lead to a better attack point just south of the control at point C

Attack points

The progression from one control to another has been described appropriately as a traffic lights situation. The first part of the section is usually uncomplicated and fast as you make your way to the nearest handrail or collecting feature; this is the green sequence. Then as you approach the end of the handrail system you enter the amber area and become cautious as you locate your selected

By deliberately aiming off about 15° to one side of a control, a fast rough compass run can be made to the catching feature, in this case the stream. Then a left turn is made, and the control is found in a few metres

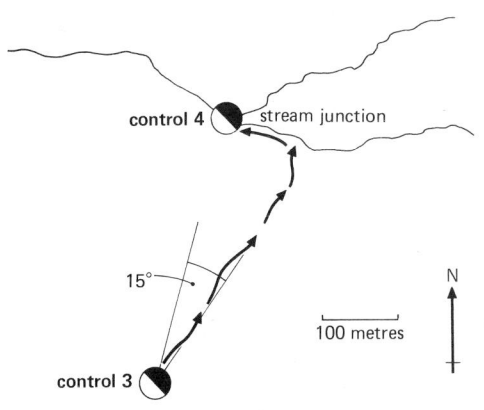

the lee of the feature. Handrails are a bonus to the orienteer who finds and uses them wisely.

Aiming off

Travel across featureless terrain on a compass bearing can be done accurately, but only very slowly. It is much better to realize that a compass course over several hundred metres is going to go adrift if undertaken coarsely at speed. A direct fast run through the forest will invariably leave you on the collecting feature with no flag in sight; then you have only a 50:50 chance of searching the correct way first time. To balance the inevitable error the orienteer aims

Relocation

If after reading this chapter so far you believe that navigation is easy, and that with skill, calmness and alertness nothing can go wrong, you are right. However, the excitement of the chase and the complexities of the forest that can never be completely displayed on the map inevitably produce times of anxiety. Blind spots, moments of inattention and lapses in concentration all conspire to get the orienteer lost. Then we find that, rather than being embraced in a friendly pattern of features that exactly match their representations on the map, we are suddenly in an alien forest where nothing resembles the marks on our piece of paper.

In situations like this, which usually happen near a control, the immediate reaction is to start hunting around in circles and darting off in all directions.

By all means look around carefully and check that you are searching for the right kind of feature – it is easy, for instance, to confuse a spur with a

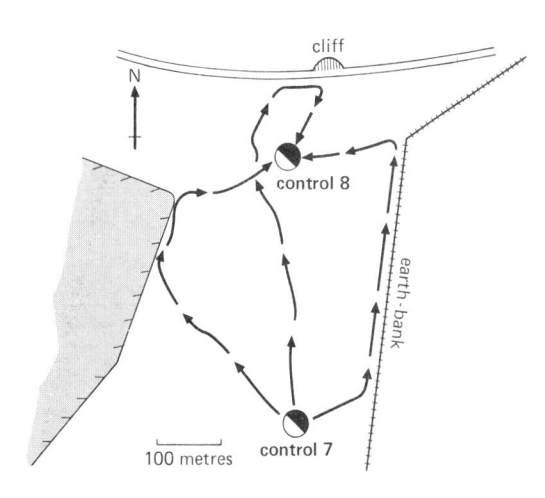

Whenever a control is on a minor non-linear feature it is best to approach it with caution from a nearby, easily located, major feature. Here are two good attack points – to the west the field corner, and to the east the earth-bank. Even a failed direct run at Control 8 will produce another attack point beyond to the north. If you fail to find the control on the way up, it is best to relocate your position accurately at the cliff and try again with care

attack point. From this feature you enter the red alert section as you navigate carefully into the control.

The key to the traffic light analogy is the attack point. An attack point must be a feature that is obvious and easily found. Features such as track junctions, field corners and major stream bends are excellent attack points, while point features such as a building, a hill summit or a pond also make suitable locations. An attack point also needs to be close to the control site – no more than 200–300 metres if it is going to be really effective. From the attack point a careful compass bearing is taken on the control, and then followed as accurately as possible while steps are counted. It is essential to be alert at this stage of a leg.

In complicated terrain, when things go wrong it is best to leave the area, identify a major feature, and start again. Here spurs and re-entrants are very similar to each other, and a lot of time could be wasted searching in the wrong places. The solution is to continue to the forestry road and make E an attack point

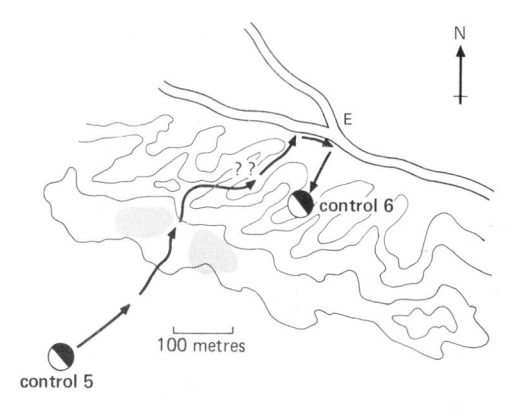

73

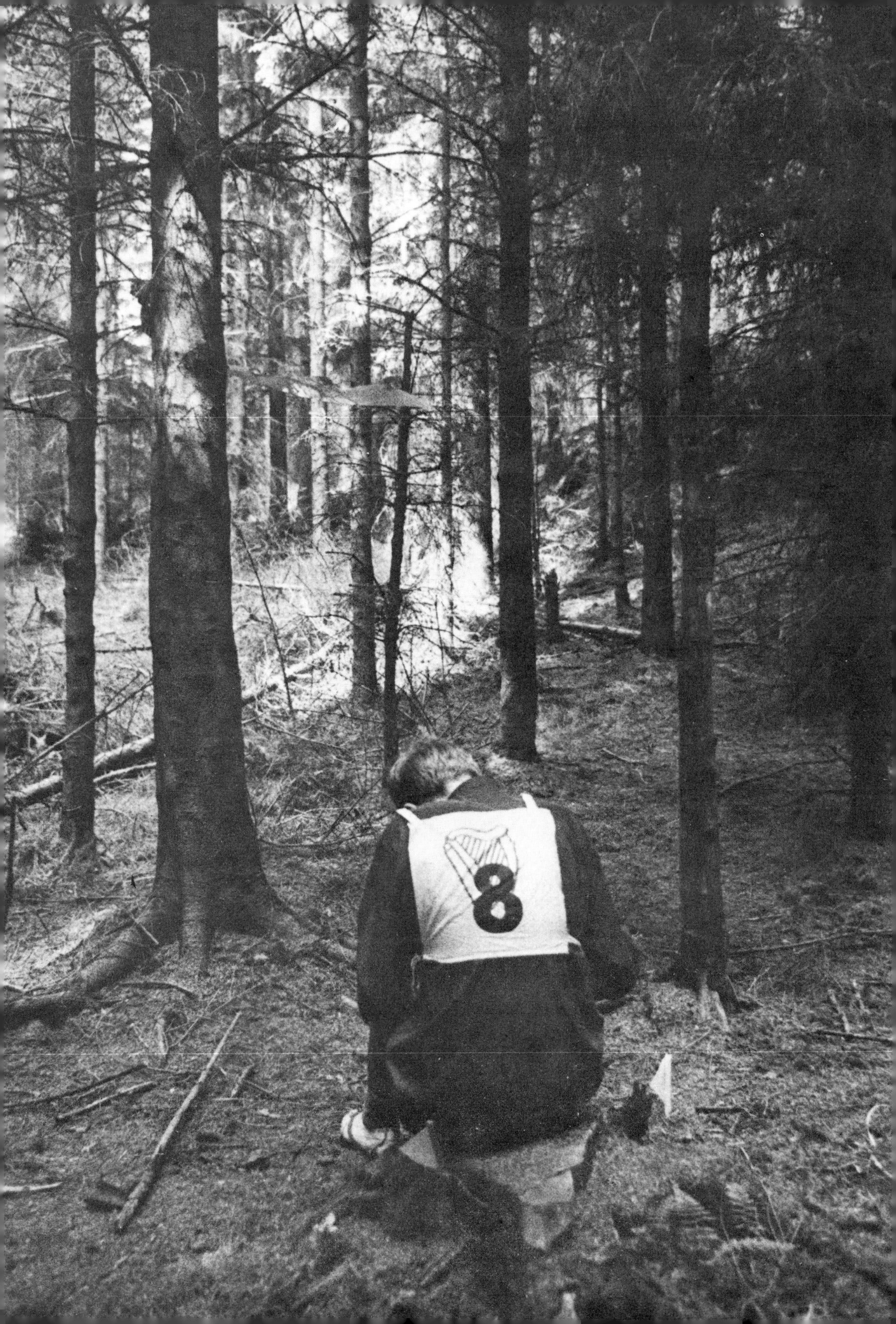

When things go wrong it can be sensible just to sit down on a log and work things out quietly before going deeper into the forest. Photo: The Times

re-entrant – but if nothing looks right don't waste time on a useless search. Get out of the area, find a recognizable major feature, and start again from a new attack point. You may well find that you have made a major error in your approach run and that you have been in the wrong parcel of forest; the sooner you find this out the better.

The beginner is often very reluctant to abandon a line of search, even though he knows deep down that he must have gone further than, say, the 150 metres he needs. It actually needs mental courage to admit that you must be wrong, and then to go and find the evidence of the error.

Mental attitudes

A positive mental approach is invaluable when confronted by navigational decisions in the forest. Even a 'wrong' decision made quickly and resolutely followed can give a better result than hesitant selection and implementation of a more technically correct route. The quickest way to finish up lost and bewildered is to dither around and lose contact with the map and ground. Once you have selected your route stick with it, and don't be distracted by external influences like other competitors or marginally attractive variations to your first choice. Obviously, though, the intelligent competitor doesn't run like a blinkered horse, and is always looking for opportunities to increase his chances. Now and again the terrain looks better in practice than was suggested by the map, and a change of plan can be made. The important point is that the change must be made in a positive way and remain part of a sound overall strategy for reaching the next control.

The beginner, and even the fairly experienced orienteer, often feels insecure when he finds himself alone in the forest, and greatly tempted to look for company and hunt in a pack. Although two heads and two pairs of eyes may seem better than one, this is only true if the other person knows what they are doing.

The rules of orienteering do not encourage following or asking advice from other competitors during a race. However, at less than championship level most events display a great deal of camaraderie: young people and hesitant beginners will usually be assisted and set on their way with new hope and their thumb on the right place on the map.

Following another competitor deliberately for several controls certainly isn't within the spirit of the sport and doesn't develop the follower's own skills. Inevitably the follower gets left high and dry and out of contact with the map, which he will have ignored. Of course there is also the distinct possibility that the 'hare' is lost himself, or on another course and looking for different controls.

However, the laws of the sport do not forbid you exercising your intelligence and knowledge of human behaviour. With experience it is quite easy to tell the difference at 30 metres between an orienteer who is still searching for the flag and one who is gleefully on his way to the next control. Similarly, you can distinguish instantly between the milling crowd of orienteers searching without hope in the wrong place, and the purposeful stream of runners being drawn to a common destination like iron filings to a magnet.

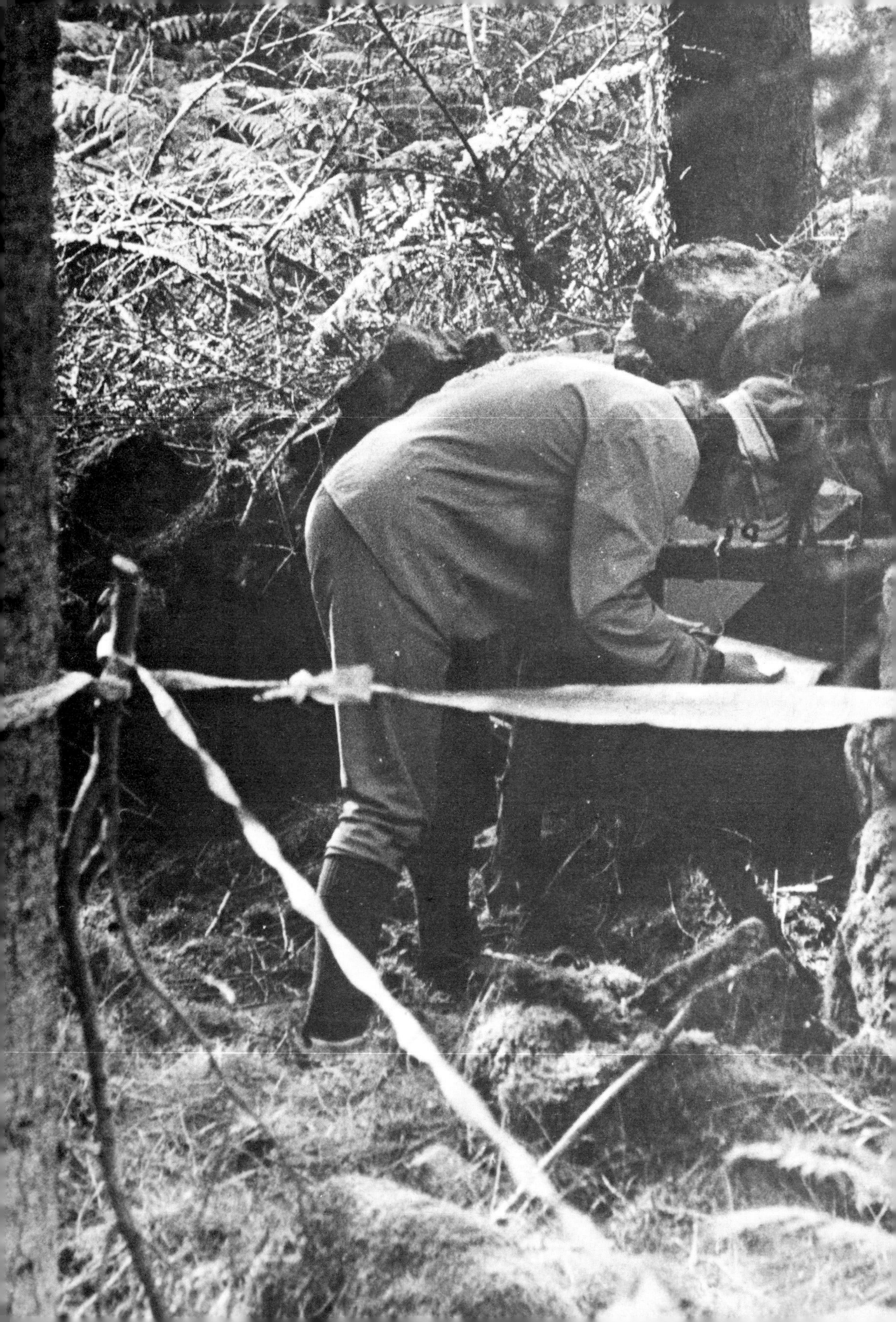

Chapter Seven
Getting Better – Additional Techniques

This chapter aims to move the beginner a little further along the road to becoming a proficient club level performer in the forest. The techniques described are for the most part an extension of the basic logic explained in the previous chapters. Their value will be recognized quickly by any orienteer who has mastered by practical application the basic elements of navigation described in Chapter 6.

The time between registration and your start can be used profitably to increase your chances of entering the forest with everything in your favour. Give yourself ample time to do all the tasks that have already been mentioned in previous chapters – don't be rushed. You need to be in a calm but purposeful frame of mind in this pre-race period. Establish a routine as soon as you can.

In the hurly-burly of the race, with the map case folded into a segment 150 × 100 millimetres and the light changing from dazzling sunshine to forest gloom, it is often difficult instantly to locate north on the map or find a north–south direction line. This problem can be reduced by, first, marking the top edge of the map with a strong band of colour, such as red, and, second, strengthening the north–south lines with a red ballpoint on sections of the map that are not likely to be used for the course – the margins, fields, dark green areas, etc.

To save time and the inconvenience of looking at two pieces of paper when

---

Checkpoint! A young orienteer clocks in.
Photo: Tom Astbury

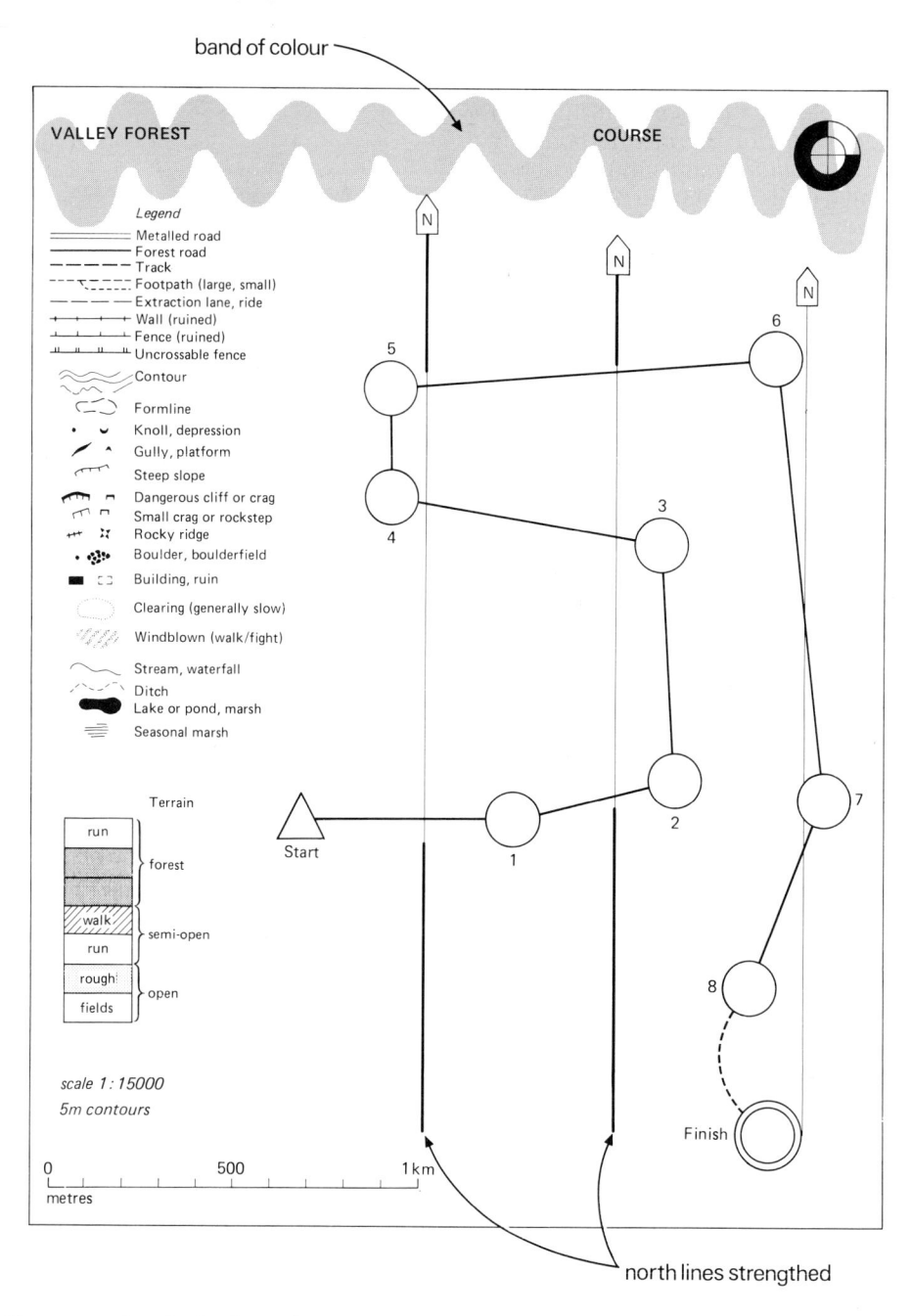

Add a strong band of colour along the north edge of the map, and strengthen the north–south lines with red ballpoint in those areas of the map which won't need to be read

Right: *Stick a small red tape arrow on the thumbnail of the hand that carries the map. This arrow directs your eye immediately to the precise spot required on the map*

It is wise to transfer the information on the control description list to the control-card if there is time before the start. This enables you to check the control code, when punching the card, without consulting another piece of paper

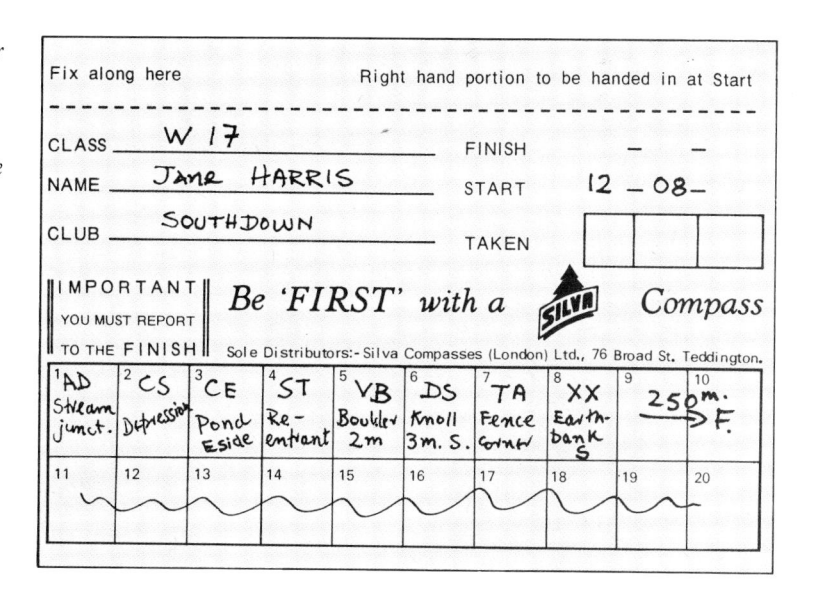

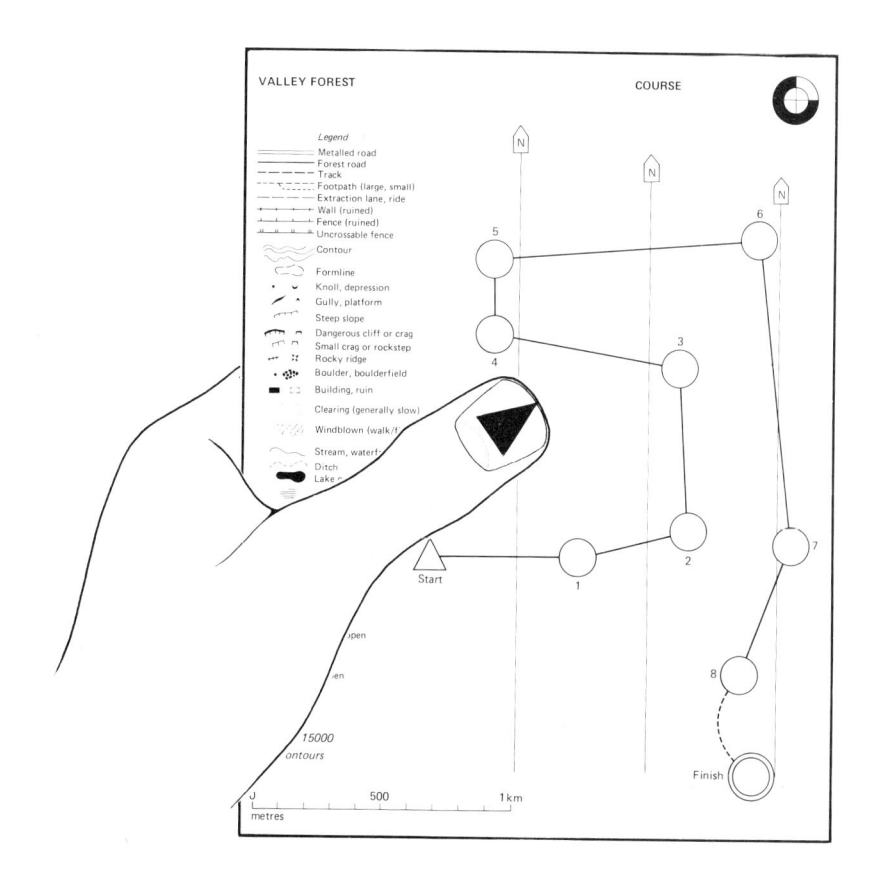

stamping at a control, it is helpful to transfer the control code and description from the control description list on to the appropriate box on the control card. But still take the description list with you as a double check.

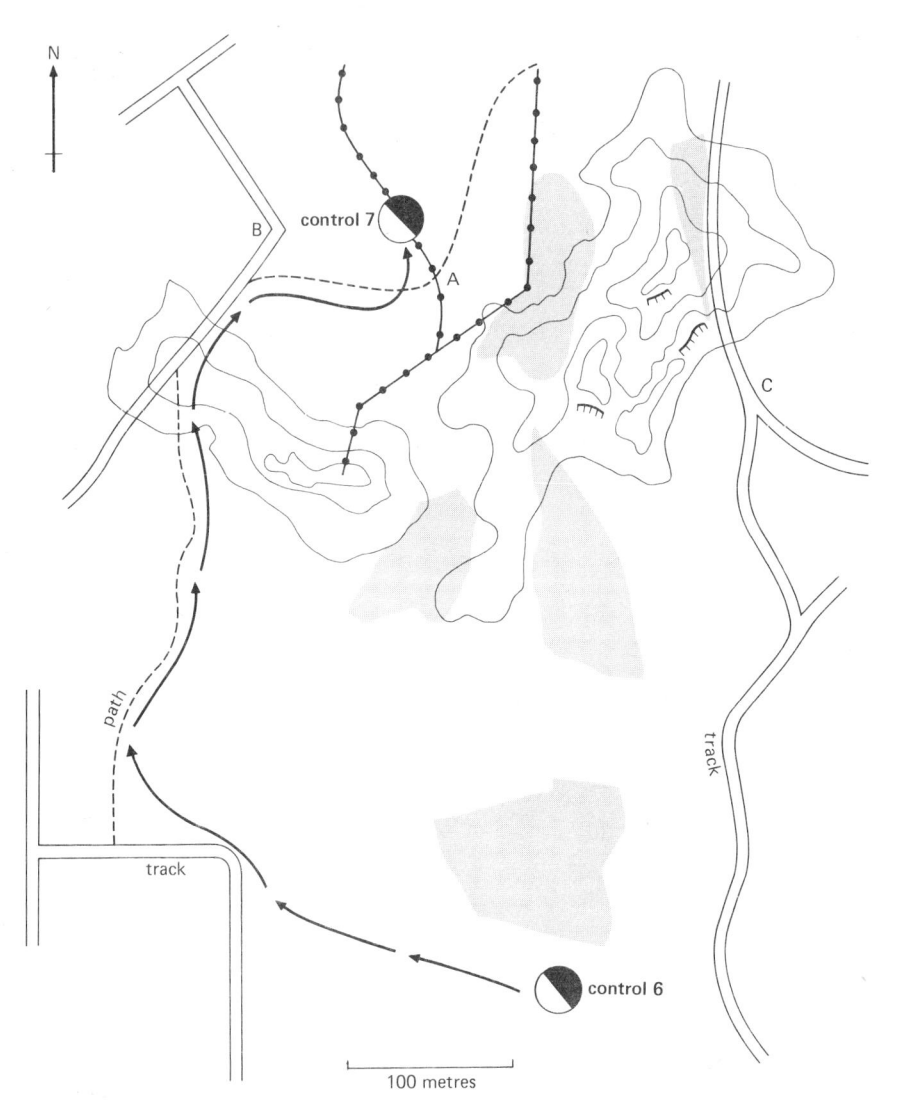

Keeping your place on the map with your thumbnail is a good way of saving a second or two every time you scrutinize the map. The thumbnail can be made more of a precision tool by sticking on a small arrow of red tape.

The aim of orienteering is to find the control features. Navigating between the controls is the means of achieving this end, so it makes good sense, particularly on the longer legs of a course, to look first for the most positive attack point. Decide on this feature and then design a fast route to reach it. This back-to-front strategy may well mean that you ignore the obvious route out of a control. Handrails that lead you to a nondescript area of forest with no prominent features may be fast, but they leave you with a headache at the end.

Left: *Here, although the forest road to the east gives almost instant access to a handrail route for two-thirds of the distance to Control 7, it eventually leaves the orienteer near point C with a very difficult final approach to the flag. The best attack points all lie to the west of the control at the path and wall crossing A or at the track corner B. This means that a westerly route is likely to be the best and fastest way of getting from 6 to 7*

There is nothing in the rules that says the orienteer shouldn't use his wits, and the sport is not called 'cunning running' for nothing. For various reasons some legs of a course sometimes produce dog legs or right-angles in the vicinity of the control feature, and these situations can often be exploited. If you can approach the control against the stream of outgoing runners from the flag there is a good chance that you will be led in to the flag. Even if you don't actually see a runner you may well, in areas of thick vegetation, see signs of their passage. These trails should lead you back into the control.

Capitalizing on the weaknesses of a course design. Right-angle turns enable you to be caught by the outgoing runners, if you approach the control from downstream. In dog leg situations, trails left through the vegetation act like pathways to the flag

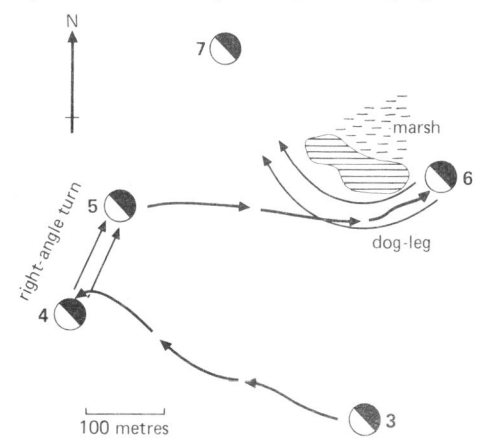

Sometimes a control is not near an attack point, typically when the control is on the far side of a bland collecting feature. Here you need to create your own attack point based on the aiming off principle. Aim off, and when you reach the collecting feature continue until

A control situated beyond an undistinguished catching feature needs a combination of aiming off and parallel travel. By hitting the forest road well to the south of Control 5 and then continuing for 90 metres an artificial attack point is created. From this point a careful compass bearing approach can be made on a course parallel to the track

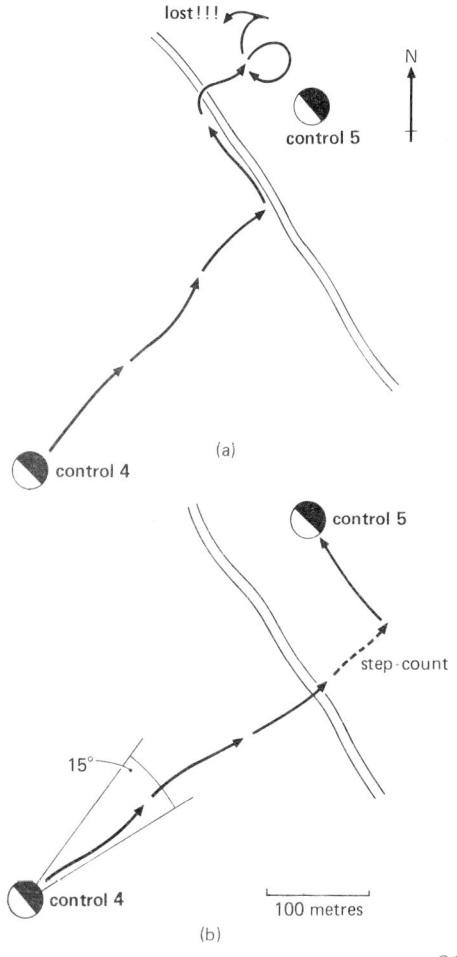

81

you reach a spot the same distance from the track as is the control. Then turn towards the control and follow a course parallel to the track until you find the flag. This technique is much faster and safer than trying to go direct to the control on a bearing, or trying to guess where to turn off the track at right-angles to the feature.

A single compass bearing will sometimes be enough to establish your position on an otherwise desolate linear feature. Relocating yourself on a long ridge or hillside can often be done quite successfully by a side bearing, but it does depend on there being a convenient feature in sight that is identifiable on both the ground and the map. Because you have good visibility from ridges and hillsides, this technique is particularly applicable in hilly country.

1. Take a visual bearing on the feature.
2. Place the long edge of the compass so that it touches the feature on the map.
3. Rotate the compass baseplate until the orienting lines in the capsule are parallel to the north–south lines on the map.
4. Your position on the hillside is where the compass edge crosses it.

This technique can be adapted to establish an attack point on a linear feature, such as a long, straight track.

1. Take a map bearing from the control to the side feature.
2. Continue along the track until the compass needle points to north, when you point the compass baseplate at the side feature. This is your attack point.

You always have better visibility looking down a slope than when looking

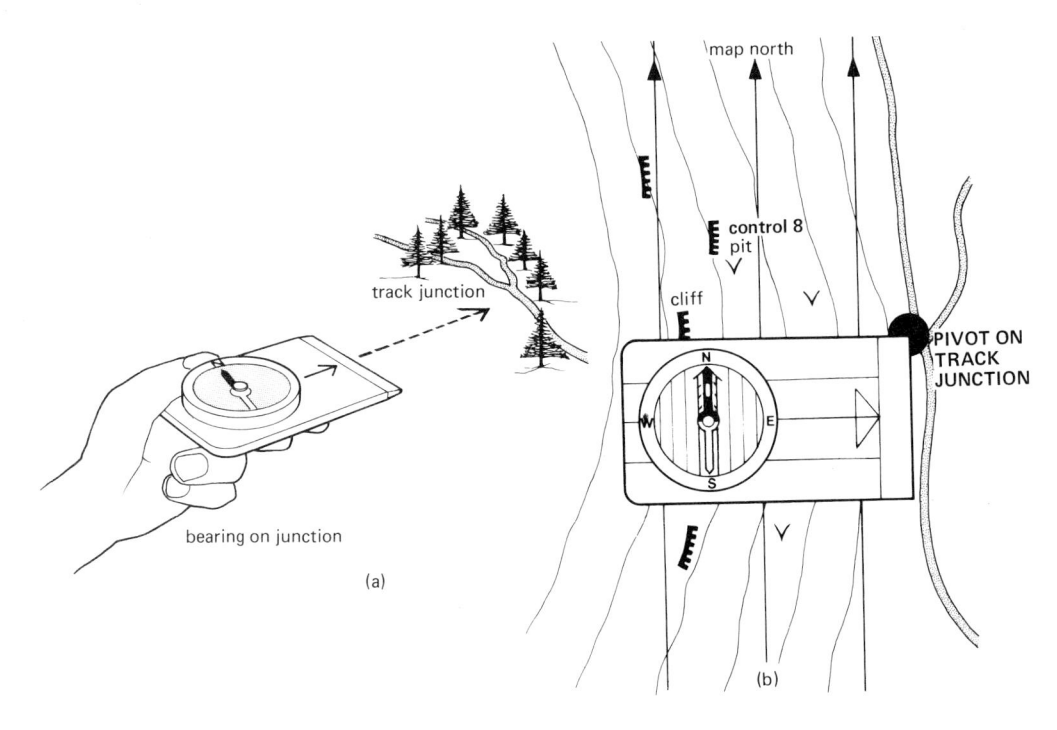

It is all too easy to get mislaid on an even-sloped hillside when searching for a control, but you can relocate yourself if you can take a fix on a recognizable feature below. Here the orienteer establishes which cliff on the hillside he is standing by when he takes a bearing (1) on the track junction in the valley. Then it is simple to find the pit at Control 8 (2)

up it. From underneath objects appear distorted, and even the physical effort of bending your neck back makes seeing difficult. Therefore if there is nothing to choose between two routes to a control on a hillside, it is better to take the high road and come down on to the control feature.

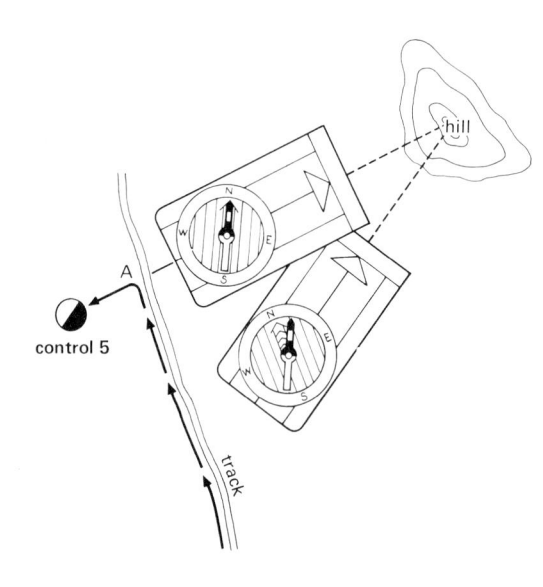

The final approach to the control is often done in company from the same attack point – the field of runners seems to concertina around the flags, and it is possible to make use of fellow competitors' vision. Assuming that another competitor is looking for the same control as you, it is worthwhile using his eyes as well as your own. This means that you should travel about 20 metres to one side and slightly behind him, because in this way you can double the frontage of the search area. If he darts off to one side you will know that he has

Above: *By taking a bearing from the map on a prominent side feature you can proceed along a linear feature until the point selected on the map (A) is reached on the ground. This can be made the attack point to reach Control 5. Point A has been reached when the compass needle points to N on the compass dial when the baseplate is pointed at the feature – the hill*

Below: *A high approach to a control gives an enhanced field of vision during the critical last 50 or so metres. When the up or down choice is more or less equal it is always sensible to descend on the control*

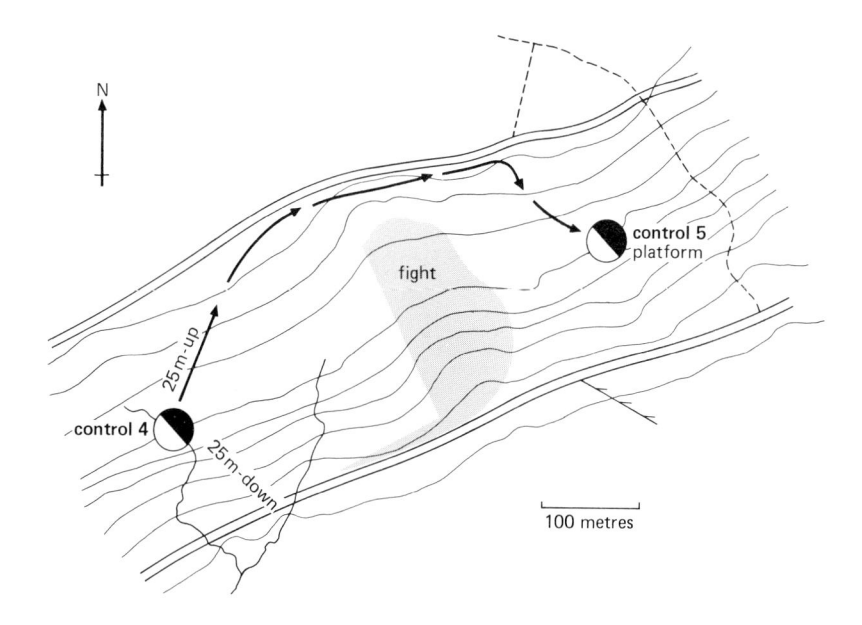

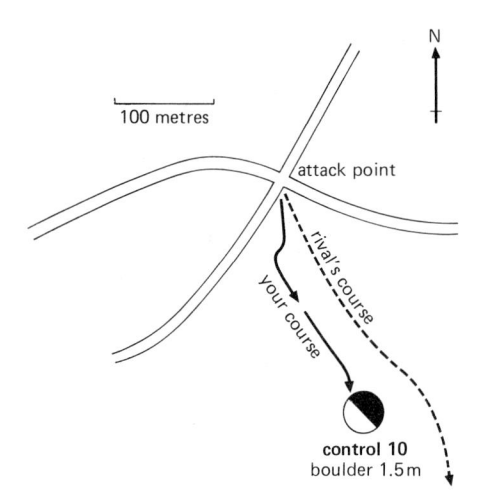

Above: *You can perfectly legitimately use a fellow orienteer's vision as well as your own if you are both approaching the control flag from the same attack point, as described in the text*

Below: *It is very easy to get disorientated at a control. Here the orienteer has come back into the control from the wrong side and has run out of the control with an 180° error. In forests with grid-like tracks this mistake won't reveal itself at the next junction, and it is only when the next control doesn't turn up that the lost orienteer finds that everything is reversed*

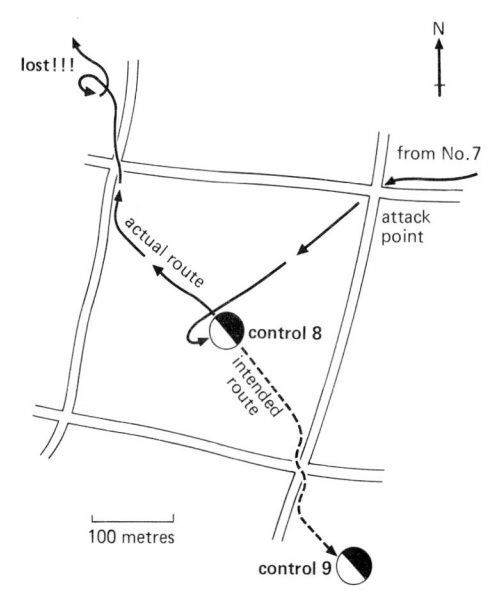

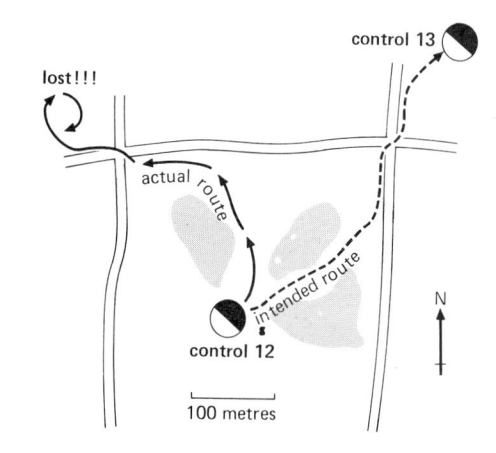

The 90° error. Here the orienteer has recognized that he needs to leave the control through a gap in thick forest, but uses the wrong corridor to reach a track. He now assumes he is travelling north and needs to cross over the next junction and swerve to the right to find the control. Again it is only when the flag doesn't appear that he consults his compass and finds he is facing north–west rather than north–east

seen the flag, and you quickly follow. If you see the red and white marker yourself, you quietly turn aside and you'll soon find out if he knows about this technique too.

Coming out of a control site after punching your card often produces major problems. First, there is a general sense of urgency to get away from the flag before you attract others to it, and second, you can easily get disorientated in your manoeuvres to get the card into the jaws of the punch. It is easy to make either a classic 180° error in direction away from the flag, or an equally frustrating 90° mistake. These blunders are particularly associated with grid-style terrain, where there are many parallel and right-angled tracks and junctions. In both cases the orienteer has not taken the time to check his compass needle, and assumes that all is well when he reaches his first crossroads of tracks. Don't be panicked out of a control. Make sure that you have the right direction, and if going to a cross-tracks, make sure that you aim off enough to one side to know exactly where you are when you hit the hard surface.

Many orienteers prefer to run with their map and compass together in one hand as a unit. They lay the compass long edge parallel and next to their intended line of travel, and then make sure that the needle points to north on the map at all times. In this way the map is set and the compass edge – or, better for visibility, an internal baseplate line – shows exactly what features will be passed over as the runner progresses. If a few seconds more are taken to twist the compass housing so that the orienting lines are parallel to the north–south lines on the map, then if you change techniques you instantly have the correct bearing to follow on the compass. This technique is exactly the same as the sequence for taking a bearing (see page 59), except that in stage 3 the compass is kept on the map when it is rotated.

Appendix One
Useful Addresses

British Orienteering Federation (BOF)

National office: 41 Dale Road, Matlock, Derbyshire, DE4 3LT

Regional orienteering associations

The BOF national office will supply an up-to-date list of addresses for the various secretaries of the regions.
Scottish Orienteering Association covers all Scotland
Welsh Orienteering Association covers all Wales
Northern Ireland Orienteering Association covers all Northern Ireland
North–West Orienteering Association Cumbria, Lancashire, Greater Manchester, Cheshire, High Peak of Derbyshire
North–East Orienteering Association Northumberland, Tyne and Wear, Durham, Cleveland
Yorkshire and Humberside Orienteering Association North Yorkshire, West Yorkshire, North Humberside, South Yorkshire
West Midlands Orienteering Association Shropshire, Staffordshire, West Midlands, Warwickshire, Hereford and Worcester
East Midlands Orienteering Association Nottinghamshire, Leicestershire, Derbyshire excluding High Peak, Lincolnshire, Northamptonshire
East Anglia Orienteering Association Norfolk, Suffolk, Cambridgeshire, Bedfordshire, Hertfordshire
South–West Orienteering Association Cornwall, Devon, Somerset, Dorset, Avon, Gloucestershire, Wiltshire
South Central Orienteering Association Hampshire, Berkshire, Oxfordshire, Buckinghamshire
South–East Orienteering Association Greater London, Surrey, Kent, West Sussex, East Sussex

Equipment suppliers

Sweat Shop, 10 The Causeway, Teddington, Middlesex, TW11 0HE (tel: 01 943 0239)
Ultrasport, The Square, Newport, Shropshire, TF10 7AG (tel: 0952 81 3918)
Runsport, 97 Barnton Street, Stirling, Scotland (tel: 0786 70694)
Running Scene, 115–117 Northumberland Street, Newcastle-upon-Tyne, Tyne and Wear (tel: 0632 29103)

Appendix Two
The BOF Badge Scheme

The scheme provides awards for proficiency assessed by a competitor's performance at certain events.

The championship badge

This is awarded annually to A class competitors who have achieved better than the winner's time plus 25 per cent in three of the following events:
1. The British Championships
2. The Jan Kjellstrom individual event
3. The four regional championships, i.e. Scottish, Northern, Midlands, Southern

A qualifying time must be achieved in either event 1 or event 2. If the Jan Kjellstrom individual is a two-day event, the combined results shall be used. A qualifying time in one age class may not count towards a badge in another class. The badge is awarded to all age classes given in BOF rule 4.1.1.

Gold, silver, bronze and iron badges

Badges are awarded on performance in championship and badge events (shown in heavy type in the national fixtures list). The scheme is open to competitors (not wayfarers) who compete on their own and reach the required standard in three events in the same class within two years.

In A classes the standards are:

Gold: better than the average of the first three competitors' times plus 25 per cent

Silver: better than the average of the first three competitors' times plus 50 per cent

Bronze: better than the average of the first three competitors' times plus 100 per cent

Iron: successful completion of the course

In B classes silver becomes plus 25 per cent, bronze plus 50 per cent and iron plus 100 per cent. In C classes bronze becomes plus 25 per cent and iron plus 50 per cent.

Should there be fewer than twenty competitors in a class who successfully complete the course, the average of the first two only is used to set the standards; if fewer than ten competitors, the winner's time alone is used. At the controller's discretion the badge scheme standard times may be adjusted where no competitor has achieved a satisfactory time.

Competitors should obtain a gold standard in their own age class before considering competing in a higher class.

A badge standard remains current for two calendar years including the year(s) in which it is achieved.

If a current gold standard competitor wishes to compete in a B class, he should enter as non-competitive and his time should not be included in the calculations.

Applying for an award

Application should be made to the BOF Badge Scheme Secretary, whose name and address are given in *The Orienteer*.

The following information should be supplied:

1. Your names and the age class in which you are claiming an award
2. The names and dates of the events concerned
3. Your position and time in each event
4. The name of your BOF club
5. Whether you wish to receive (a) brooch badge, (b) cloth badge, (c) certificate (prices are given in *The Orienteer*)

Send a crossed postal order or cheque made payable to British Orienteering Federation, together with a stamped addressed envelope, minimum size 28 × 22 centimetres, for the certificate. Age flashes, i.e. W 10 to W 56 and M 10 to M 56, are also available (prices in *The Orienteer*).

Appendix Three
Additional Technical Information

How to construct your own step scale

The following equation gives millimetres per 100 steps:

$$\frac{10,000,000}{\text{Map scale} \times \text{steps per 100 metres}}$$

For example, an orienteer with a 36-step rate to the 100 metres, working with a 1:15,000 map, will have the following result:

$$\frac{10,000,000}{15,000 \times 36}$$

= 18.5 millimetres per 100 steps

Bearings from a non-orienteering map

Orienteers often compete in some of the mountain and fell-running events that

Using the compass as a protractor on an Ordnance Survey map. Join the trig. point and the church with the long edge of the compass (1). Twist the compass housing until N on the dial is to the north edge of the map (orienting lines parallel to the grid lines). Lift the compass off the map, hold it close to your chest, then turn your body and the compass round until the red needle points to 353° on the dial (2). Look up and you are facing the church

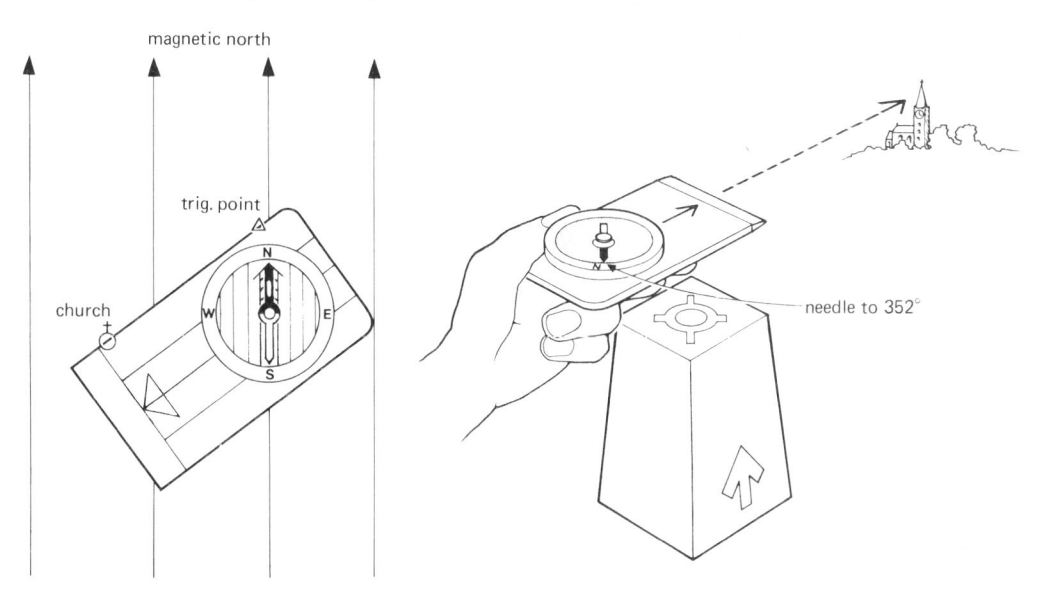

require navigation. These events, such as the Lake District Mountain Trial and the Karrimor and Saunders Mountain Marathons, usually rely on Ordnance Survey maps, which means that competitors need to realize that map north is not synonymous with compass north, and to take appropriate action when taking bearings.

The following simple technique avoids any difficulties arising from additions and substractions and when to do them.

1. Take all bearings from the map in the normal manner.

2. Whenever you use the compass needle to take a bearing, have it point to 353° and not to north (360°) on the compass housing. It is helpful to stick a slim arrow of white stamp edging on the bottom of the capsule to mark this 353° line.

NB Magnetic north is about 7° west of grid north in Great Britain at the present time.

Appendix Four
Glossary

Aiming off A vital technique used for finding point features situated on linear features. It involves deliberately going to one side of the point and then turning towards the point when the linear feature is reached.

Attack point An easily located feature within a few hundred metres of the control. A careful compass course is taken from the attack point to the flag.

Back bearing The reverse direction to the bearing, and found by swinging the compass so that the south end of the compass needle points to north on the dial.

Bearing The direction of travel as found from the map and indicated by the compass.

Beck See *stream*.

Bog See *marsh*.

Boulder A stone higher than 1 metre.

Boulder field An area containing many boulders, too numerous to be shown individually on the map.

Brook See *stream*.

Burn See *stream*.

Catching agent See *collecting feature*.

Clearing An area in the forest with no trees, but not a felled area.

Cliff See *crag*.

Collecting feature An easily recognized linear feature at right-angles to the orienteer's direction of travel.

Contouring The technique of traversing around or across a slope without gaining or losing height.

Contour line A line on the map that indicates all the points that are the same height above sea level.

Contour interval The difference in height between adjacent contour lines.

Control One of several locations in the forest that the orienteer visits during an event. It is indicated on the map by a red circle and on the ground by a red and white prism marker.

Control card Usually a piece of card, but can be an integral part of the map, on which are numbered boxes in which marks are made to record the finding of the appropriate controls.

Control punch A device attached to or near the control flag, that makes a distinctive mark when closed on the appropriate box on the control card.

Crag A rock up to 2 metres high. See also *dangerous crag*.

Dangerous crag A rock more than 2 metres high.

Declination The angle between the direction to which the compass needle points and true north. Only of interest to the orienteer when using maps drawn to grid north; orienteering maps are always drawn to magnetic north.

Depression A natural hollow (higher ground on all sides). Small features are shown with a brown U symbol; large (in area) features with form lines with internal tags.

Description sheet The list of controls which indicates various facts about the controls and the course. It is usually a separate piece of paper, but for important events is printed on the map.

Ditch Refers to the man-made article, usually wet; a ditch which is usually dry may be shown as a *small gully*.

Dog legs Part of the course where incoming and outgoing runners use the same route.

Dry ditch See *small gully*.

Form line An additional contour line that helps the mapmaker convey the exact form of the feature. It is depicted by a broken brown line.

Handrails Prominent linear features such as tracks, paths, walls, fences and power lines, which guide the orienteer through the forest.

Hill 5–20 metres high (ring contour).

Knoll A small hill 1–5 metres high (brown symbol). See also *rocky knoll*.

Large gully See *ravine*.

Leg The part of the course between adjacent controls.

Legend See *map symbols*.

Linear feature A line feature which has enough length to be of use to the orienteer either as a collecting feature or as a handrail.

Magnetic lines Lines drawn from north to south on the orienteering map, and usually placed 500 metres apart.

Map corrections Official maps displayed near the registration point which record any necessary alterations that should be made to the competitors' maps before going to the start.

Map symbols The various designs and devices that indicate the features of the landscape; sometimes called the legend.

Marsh Very wet ground, with or without trees. See also *seasonal marsh* and *uncrossable marsh*.

Master maps The official true record of the situation of the controls on any course; they are visited by the orienteer immediately after the start.

Niche A very small re-entrant, usually narrow, and shown by a bend in one contour or form line.

Orientate The process of arranging the map so that it is aligned with the corresponding features on the ground; also called setting the map.

Outcrop See *crag*.

Pace scale See *step scale*.

Pacing See *step count*.

Pit A small, steep-sided hollow, usually man-made (brown V symbol). Large (in area) features, e.g. sand quarries, are shown with a steep slope symbol, i.e. brown comb. See also *rocky pit*.

Platform A small, level area on a slope.

Point features Small features in the forest, such as knolls, depressions, ruins, ponds and boulders, which are often used as control sites.

Precision compass The technique used to locate a control by taking a careful bearing from the map and then selecting the route ahead with precision.

Pulpit See *platform*.

Rack A narrow ride 3–5 metres wide, usually in series spaced 10–30 metres apart, e.g. line thinning.

Ravine A line feature more than 2 metres deep, and difficult to cross.

Re-entrant A small valley without a permanent watercourse.

Registration The place where entries on the day are accepted, and maps, control cards and description sheets are obtained in exchange for the fee.

Ride A clearly visible linear gap in the forest, more than 5 metres wide; a firebreak.

River A watercourse wider than 5 metres.

Rock See *crag*.

Rocky knoll A knoll consisting mainly of bare rock.

Rocky pit A depression, usually man-made, with steep, rocky sides (black V symbol).

Rough compass The technique used to progress through the forest by just noting the general direction in respect to the compass needle.

Scree An area carrying many stones, mainly smaller than boulder size.

Seasonal marsh A marsh that is not wet during dry summer weather, but vegetation (usually rushes) is indicative of wetness.

Setting the map See *orientate*.

Small gully A line feature, not necessarily straight, more than 0.5 metres deep, and easy to cross.

Spur A small ridge, usually steep and subsidiary to the main ridge.

Start lines A corridor system by which the competitors advance by a minute countdown process to the actual starting line. The system is usually based on a three- to four-minute timescale.
Step See *crag*.
Step count The counting of double steps which helps the orienteer measure distance on the ground fairly accurately.
Step scale A special scale that relates pace length to distance on the map. Instead of recording distance the step scale gives the number of paces.
Stream See *marsh*.
Swamp See *marsh*.
Terrace See *platform*.
Thicket An area of dense forest, difficult to cross.
Thumbing Keeping the thumbnail directly on the place on the map where the orienteer now is; a red tape arrow head is often stuck on the thumbnail to help precision.
Uncrossable marsh A marsh that is dangerous to cross.
Vegetation boundary A distinct change in forest type, e.g. trees of different species or height.
Wayfaring Special courses that are attractive to the non-competitive navigator or to families with small children.

Position of the marker

The position of the marker with reference to the feature it is on is often a necessary piece of information. The terms used to describe that position are listed below. Where appropriate they will be supplemented by points of the compass, e.g. north side, south–east edge.
Bend At the bend of a linear feature, e.g. path, track, ride, stream, ditch, wall, fence.
Corner Used to describe edges of areas, e.g. field, felled area.
Edge On the border of an area, e.g. marsh, clearing, felled area.
Foot At the base of a steep feature, e.g. crag, steep slope.
Junction Where linear features join or cross.
Part A site in the centre of a distinct section of a marsh, clearing, felled area etc.
Side Beside a feature which rises above ground, e.g. boulder, knoll, thicket.

NB Where two or more similar features lie within the control circle on the map, the control feature is indicated in the description as the northern, southern, etc., of two, or northmost, etc., of more than two.

Appendix Five
IOF Control Description Symbols

example

H17-18A	9·8km	400m				
1	64		≡			▶
2	36	↗	•		2	○
3	39		⊌	U		○
4	61		m			
5	49	▯◦▯	▲		1·5	⊙ θ
6	40					
○ — — 350m — — ○						
ʌ ʌ ʌ ʌ ʌ ʌ ʌ						
A B C D E F G H						

class (H17 – 18A)
course length (9·8 km)
climbing (400 metres)
controls:
1. code number 64
   marsh, east corner
2. code number 36
   northeastern knoll
   height 2 metres
   southeastern foot
and so on
route from the last
control to the finish
(350 metres, all marked)

Key to the columns
A control number
B control code
C which feature (or any similar ones)
D the control feature
E details of appearance
F dimensions of the control feature
G location of the marker
H other information

Some combinations
columns C, D

| •| ⌀ | between the hills |
| •| ⌀ | between knoll and hill |

columns D, E, F

⤫	ditch junction
⊲ ⊠	clump of deciduous trees
	path/ride crossing
↝ ↝	stream/ditch junction
⊗ •|	tree root on ride
⌣ ※	depression north of thicket
▲ ⌐	boulder on spur

column C
↑	northern
↗	northeastern
⤒	upper
⤓	lower
▯◦▯	middle
•|•	between

column D
•	knoll
○	hill
)(	saddle
][	pass
▷	terrace
▶	spur
⫞⫞⫞	rib
⋂	re-entrant
∧	gully
⌣	small depression
⊖	depression
⌐	cliff
▲	boulder
▲▲▲	boulder field
<	cave
∨	pit
⊡	quarry
⊖	gravel pit
⤊	steep bank
⊢⊢⊢	boundary bank

column D (continued)
■	building
⌑	ruin
⊤	tower
⊥	fodder rack
⊙	cairn
⌬	lake
⌬	pond
⌣	waterhole
○	well
⌇	source
↯	stream
⇝	ditch
⤳	dry ditch
≡	small marsh
≣	marsh
※	thicket
⋯	clearing
⋰	vegetation boundary
⊗	tree root
⊲	copse
◁	single tree
∕	ride
⸝	path
∕	road
⤫	bridge
↯	fence
⤨	wall

column E
⌣	shallow
⋃	deep
※	overgrown
⋯	open
⚘	coniferous
⊣	end
<	bend
⋋	junction
⨯	crossing

column F
| 2·2 | height in metres |
| 6x5 | length/width in metres |

column G
↺	northern side
↻	northwest edge
▷	east corner (inside the angle)
⊥	southwest corner
⋎	southern tip
⊙	western part
▯•▯	upper part
⋔	on the top of
⚲	southern foot
⌊	the foot (direction unspecified)

column H
⊕	refreshments
⚡	radio control
⚐	manned control

© 1980 Harvey Map Services Ltd

94

Appendix Six
Permanent Wayfaring Courses

If you would prefer to experiment with a map and compass in private, away from the turmoil of an actual event, and iron out the bugs from your navigational system before going in for a competition, it can be arranged. With the co-operation of local orienteering clubs, the Forestry Commission and several other forest owners have marked out permanent courses in some thirty forests in Britain. These particular forests have been selected because of their accessibility and their attractiveness to the rambler who leaves the beaten track.

The map

These are proper orienteering maps with the correct symbols for features, and with a scale of either 1:10,000 or 1:15,000 (approximately 6 inches and 4 inches to the mile respectively). The maps can be bought from the forest office; ring the appropriate telephone number from the list that follows. The forests are usually open during daylight hours.

The course

You can devise your own circuit from the twenty or so control points marked and described on the map. The actual markers are not the usual prism flags but a coloured marker post with a code letter or number. An example of the control is often displayed in the car parking area.

A family outing

The wayfaring forests are in wonderful country and will make an ideal expedition for the family. Not only can you navigate to the controls, but you can also locate viewpoints, waterfalls, lakes and picnic sites. Take a packed lunch and have a day out. You can also organize competitions by picking different routes to a control and seeing which one is the quickest, or devising a small circuit and timing yourself or members of your group or family around the course. Compasses would be helpful in wayfaring forests, but they are not essential as the control sites are on obvious features and the chosen forests reasonably open.

Wayfaring courses in Britain

England

Hamsterly Forest, Durham (0207 520473)
Dalby Forest, Pickering, North Yorkshire (0904 769290)
Strenshall Common, North Yorkshire (0904 769290)
Ilkley Moor, Ilkley, West Yorkshire (0943 601124)
Ennerdale, Cumbria (0946 811130)
Lyme Park, Manchester (060 430 2003)
Primrose Hill, Chester (024 450 344)
Clent Hills, Hereford and Worcester (021 354 3893)
Downs Bank, Stone, Staffordshire (063 087 2827)
Cannock Chase, Lichfield, Staffordshire (054 32 52082)
Shotover Woods, Oxfordshire (0235 20930)
Ashton Court, Bristol (0272 664169)
Crowthorne Woods, Bracknell, Berkshire (042 128 2801)
Hampstead Heath, London (01 445 3106)

Ranmore Common, Dorking, Surrey
(0372 52528)
Forest of Dean, Monmouth, Gwent
(0272 713471)
Queen Elizabeth Country Park,
Petersfield, Hampshire (0705 595040)
Whippendell Woods, Watford,
Hertfordshire (0923 43724)
Whinlatter Forest, Cumbria
(059 682 469)
Chiltern Forest, Buckinghamshire
(084 44 6474)

Wales

Gwydwr Forest, Penmachno, Gwynedd
(0492 640578)
Beddgelert Forest, Beddgelert, Gwynedd
(0492 640578)

Afan Argoed, Port Talbot, West
Glamorgan (0792 23515)
Llanrisant Forest, Cardiff (0222 40661)
Westwood, Newport, Gwent
(0222 40661)
Singleton Park, Swansea (0792 23515)

Scotland

Queens Forest, Aviemore, Inverness-
shire (0463 32811)
Kirkhill Forest, Aberdeen, Grampian
(0224 33361)
Beecraigs, Edinburgh (050 684 3121)
Glentress Forest, Peebles (0721 20373)

Northern Ireland

Hillsborough Forest (0846 682477)